A. J. SHERMAN

My Oxford

My Oxford

MARTIN AMIS NINA BAWDEN JOHN BETJEMAN
LORD BOOTHBY ALAN COREN ANTONIA FRASER
JO GRIMOND RAYMOND MASSEY JOHN MORTIMER
NIGEL NICOLSON J.I.M.STEWART ANGUS WILSON

Edited and introduced by
ANN THWAITE

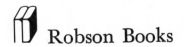 Robson Books

FIRST PUBLISHED IN GREAT BRITAIN IN 1977
BY ROBSON BOOKS LTD., 28 POLAND STREET,
LONDON W1V 3DB. COPYRIGHT © 1977 ROBSON
BOOKS.

ISBN 0 903895 83 8

Illustrations by Sylvia Hall from *Introducing Oxford*,
copyright Lise Millar and Sylvia Hall.

Endpapers show (front) the Radcliffe Camera and (back)
a view of St Mary's Church, All Souls, University and
Queen's Colleges, and are reproduced by courtesy of
Oxfordshire County Libraries.

Printed in Great Britain by R. J. Acford Ltd., Chichester

CONTENTS

INTRODUCTION

In an agreeable letter turning down an invitation to contribute to this book, Lindsay Anderson looked back at his
time at Oxford and wrote, 'I haven't particularly golden
memories of the period—and I am not altogether in favour of
perpetuating the Oxbridge myth.' Of course, this book *is* full
of stories, of myths. J. I. M. Stewart attached a note to his piece
saying, 'At least it's a monument of veracity: not a fib from
beginning to end', but it is rather difficult to believe in the
Provost of Oriel and his use of Sir Thomas Browne and the
badger to speed his parting guests. Nor am I entirely convinced
by John Betjeman's Lecturer in Spanish who did not think
Spanish a language worth studying. Did C. S. Lewis really
wonder whether Coleridge's pants were woollen or fur? Did
J. M. Barrie really crawl out of a fireplace? Is it a fact that the
Bywater and Sotheby Professor of Byzantine and Modern
Greek had once been an electrical engineer in Chelmsford?
(The Bywater and Sotheby Professor of my own day is now,
far more probably, the Greek Minister of Culture.)

But many stories have the ring of truth: the Lord Chancellor
of England being called a saucy boy, Rudyard Kipling timing
the Balliol boat at Henley, the Hertford don declaring 'I do
not lecture to *undergraduettes*'; so too have Nina Bawden's
strange tea party with Richard Burton and her argument with
Margaret Thatcher. And Angus Wilson goes out of his way to

dispel a myth, to explain how it came about that a don's wife said to him recently, 'I hear you spent nearly all your time at Oxford dressed as a woman.' We are perpetuating myths and telling good stories; we are also communicating some truths.

One truth that hardly needs stating is that everyone's Oxford is different. As things turned out, I have ended up with three Balliol men among my contributors and a rather excessive number of historians. Lord Boothby and Raymond Massey were up at the same time, so were John Betjeman and J. I. M. Stewart, and so, in the mid-'thirties, were Angus Wilson and Jo Grimond. But one would hardly guess this from reading their pieces. Their Oxfords were each entirely distinct. At any one time, there are circles in Oxford which never touch or overlap. I did try not to give the impression that Oxford produces nothing but politicians and professional writers, and I'm glad to have an actor and a lawyer. But it is a pity I could not persuade a scientist to contribute.

People's memories are strange things: there are bound to be odd errors and falsifications in this book, as well as exaggerations and deliberate distortions. In Peter Quennell's recent autobiography he says how flattered and amazed he was to read Graham Greene's tribute to his schoolboy prowess on a horse: 'Quennell always rode a far more spirited horse than mine, galloped faster, jumped higher.' 'In fact,' says Quennell, 'the hack I rode was by no means spirited; and I have seldom taken a jump if it could possibly be ridden round.' I am sure there are examples of this sort of thing in these pages.

This is in no way a comprehensive study of Oxford from the end of the first world war to the present day. There are many gaps, in time and activity. One such is sport. There is a good deal of rowing but not much else. I myself can do little to remedy that omission. Table tennis was the only game I played for my college. I did once see Oxford play the New Zealanders at rugby but my most vivid sporting memory is of hearing, from inside St Hilda's, the roar that went up from the Iffley Road sports ground the moment that Roger Bannister broke the four-minute mile. I never saw Colin Cowdrey play and I didn't particularly want to meet him after reading, in his *Isis* Idol, that his chief hobbies were sleep and eating oranges.

There are a number of names I would have liked to see in these pages. Others recur often. F. F. Urquhart, Dean of Balliol, crops up again and again. I was amused to read in Anthony Powell's *Infants of the Spring* that my contributors are apparently guilty of a solecism. Powell writes sternly that it is 'not Sligger Urquhart, as now sometimes altogether incorrectly rendered, but either Sligger or Urquhart.' After reading the varied descriptions of Urquhart in these pages, it might interest anyone to know that his alleged vices apparently excited Evelyn Waugh to shout in the quad at dead of night: 'The Dean of Balliol sleeps with men!'

It is the dons, of course, that give Oxford its continuity. The undergraduates come and go very quickly but a don may be there, in one form or another, for more than half a century. R. H. Dundas was already Senior Censor at Christ Church in the 'twenties. Thirty years later he was still, in Boothby's phrase, 'asking undergraduates rather intimate questions about their private lives'. College servants, too, give continuity. The chef at Magdalen, referred to by Lord Boothby, was living in retirement in Cowley Place when I was up. His name was Mr Duke and he would remember with affection Oscar Wilde and the Prince of Wales, Lord Boothby and Mr Hodder (of Hodder and Stoughton). My fiancé and the present editor of *The Times Literary Supplement* had rooms in his house, and it was Mrs Duke who insisted on serving them such mammoth breakfasts (porridge, kippers, mashed potatoes, liver, bacon and eggs, etc) that they were forced to deposit packets of unwanted food each morning in the litter basket on Magdalen Bridge.

Lord Boothby's conversation with Sir Herbert Warren is also the sort of thing to fuel the anger of anyone who thinks of Oxford as a den of nepotism, privilege and gracious over-eating. In the 'fifties, at least in the limited circles in which I moved, we had no hang-ups about the ancient universities. We knew anyone could get in who had the brains and determination. Certainly no one I knew avoided them for egalitarian reasons, as the young do nowadays, opting very often for Sussex or York or the University of East Anglia, as being in some mysterious way more like real life. Of course, the new universities did not exist. The alternatives were Bristol, Leeds, Manchester and so on.

I was going to Cambridge, and had indeed already accepted a place at Newnham, when the St Hilda's offer came and I decided, in a flash, that I would rather go to Oxford. I rationalized the important decision in various ways: Newnham was large and had television in one JCR (both cons), St Hilda's was small and was on the river. Moreover, St Hilda's had the formidably impressive Helen Gardner, whose combination of T. S. Eliot and the metaphysicals pleased me. (I had by some extraordinary oversight not realized that *she* was to examine me when I presented as part of my entrance papers a feeble version of her own *Art of T. S. Eliot*. Nor had I really taken in the fact that Eliot, or indeed anyone later than 1830, played no part whatsoever in the English Schools syllabus at the time.)

More cogent really than these outward reasons was the effect of some recent reading: most particularly Spender's *World Within World* and, inevitably, *Brideshead Revisited*. (I was surprised when re-reading that recently to find how much of it is not about Oxford.) Auden and Louis MacNeice were my favourite poets. Of my interview visit to Oxford (sunny, crisp, where Cambridge had been misty, moist), my strongest memory is of my pleasure in finding a signed copy of MacNeice's *Plant and Phantom* in Blackwell's. Antonia Fraser's Oxford is closest to my own. I went up in her last year. I belonged to the Experimental Theatre Club and wore black gaberdine trousers and a black polo-necked sweater. I carried a Goray skirt with my gown in my bicycle bag ready for a quick change before dining in hall. The great thing was to avoid bearing any resemblance either to the earnest females in 'hairy woollens and shapeless tweeds' of Christopher Hobhouse's Batsford book on Oxford (how we hated his description of the women's colleges) or to the 'twittering and fluttering' female intruders of *Brideshead*.

We were not like that at all. There were ten of us reading English at St Hilda's in our year and it included two really beautiful girls: Gillian Palmer and Sally Philipps. In a recent profile of her husband, Michael Frayn, Gill was described as 'once an Oxford belle', a phrase to make anyone shudder and Gill most of all. She has remained, for twenty-five years, one of my closest friends. Both Gill and Sally had more than beauty. Charisma is, I suppose, the current word for it. Sally became the wife of P. J. Kavanagh and, after her early death, *The Perfect Stranger* of his book. Sally's mother was Rosamond Lehmann, then at the height of her fame as a novelist. Her father was a communist, Wogan Philipps, then heir to Lord Milford. By strange coincidence, through the CP, he had known Ruth Mitchell's father, a shop steward in a West Midlands factory. Ruth was perhaps the dominant figure in our group (a word we used before Mary McCarthy's novel)—atheistic, argumentative, touchy, loyal and kind, she went on to marry first a bisexual mathematician who killed himself and then a black civil rights lawyer in Los Angeles. She never did do things the easy way.

Like Angus Wilson, like most people, I had my social horizons widened by Oxford. Like him, I had rarely met anyone before from north of Watford. Although I had not led a particularly sheltered existence, I now found myself for the first time talking to Etonians, homosexuals and Bradford chemists. Beneath the shimmering surface—the white wine in punts tied up beneath the willows, the black Russian cigarettes (the same kind Stewart bought thirty years before) smoked by firelight in old rooms—I became aware of dark things affecting people I knew: abortion, betrayal, suicide. When I saw for the first time that startling epitaph in the abbey at Dorchester just outside Oxford, I knew that what I often suffered gladly was the burden of 'excessive sensibility'. For me it brought not death but a mild rebuke from my Principal, Miss Mann: 'One's first summer term often goes to one's head.'

Our mantelpieces were loaded with invitations—printed, crested, comforting. They came from men in suits. Many of them, like Martin Amis fifteen years later, were spending a lot of time not getting girl friends. When they did get them, they were not always sure what to do with them. In Philip Larkin's preface to *Jill*, he recalls walking down the High after the war, seeing an undergraduate in a sky-blue cloak with hair down to his shoulders, and realizing that all that was starting again. Perhaps he had seen Ken Tynan, who had gone down before I went up. 'Never wear a tweed coat and flannel trousers,' Charles Ryder had been told. And there was George MacBeth in a neat suit with *spats*. Velvet corduroy jackets were all right, and many people wore coloured waistcoats with brass buttons from Halls, close cousins of the ones Angus Wilson mentions. Tweed sports coats were only for the trogs, like the college scarves Antonia Fraser mentions. I actually bought a college scarf before I realized it was not the thing. I don't think I ever wore it at Oxford but it comes in very useful now on occasions (many) when I prefer to be warm rather than elegant. What a snobbish lot we were. Our snobbery had nothing to do with money or birth but everything to do with intellect and style.

I saw George MacBeth in my first week at Oxford, at the first meeting of the Poetry Society. He was Secretary, and stood on the platform beside Dylan Thomas in the packed, enthralled Rhodes House. Alan Coren says of his time, 'Poetry, or Dom Moraes as it came to be called . . .' In my time, poetry had many names. I found a note in my 1953 diary predicting the four poets of our generation. (Four because we always thought of Auden, MacNeice, Spender and Day Lewis bracketed together for the 'thirties.) 'Geoffrey Hill, Thom Gunn, Anthony Thwaite and Alistair Elliot,' I wrote. I had not then heard of Ted Hughes, who was at Cambridge at the time, like Gunn. There were plenty of other contenders: Alan Brownjohn, Adrian Mitchell, Edward Lucie-Smith, George

MacBeth, Jonathan Price. No women. I stopped writing poetry (and my diary) soon after this.

I was eventually Treasurer of the Poetry Society. It was not a sinecure. In fact, it still owes me £20. That was a lot of money at a time when the Regency, Long John's restaurant in St Giles, served an excellent dinner at a maximum price of nine shillings. It was an impossible task balancing subscriptions against the cost of providing quantities of terrible sherry for the pre-meeting party, meals at the Café de Paris, and a poet's bedroom at the Mitre. Sometimes there were disputes about whether we should pay for the poet's wife or mistress as well. Our bank balance was swelled by Spender and Claire Bloom at successive meetings. For her we even had rugby players queuing up to pay their subscriptions. But other occasions, such as the visit of Jocelyn Brooke, and John Wain on 'Deadlock in contemporary poetics,' were definitely for the minority.

Apart from parties and poetry, for me there was *Isis* and the theatre. I wrote a lot for *Isis* and spent much time in the little office in Alfred Street, deciding on type-faces and pasting up galleys. I ended up as Features Editor. Jo Grimond writes very casually that he edited it. In our day, it was certainly a major commitment. Tutors had to give permission and expected no essays that term. As for 'theatre', we were invited to read in plays all the time: *Edward II* at New College one night, *The Way of the World* at Balliol another, *Juno and the Paycock* at Trinity, *Rain* at Pembroke, *Dear Brutus* at Univ. It was not surprising that I soon felt acquainted with a fair proportion of the undergraduate population. There were more nerve-wracking debating invitations too, supporting Jeremy Isaacs at Merton, opposing Nemone Lethbridge at Lincoln. But acting was best.

When I was Myra in *Hay Fever*, Vernon Dobtcheff described me in *Isis* as 'witty, mature, sepulchrally enjoying a dumpy languor'. I wasn't quite happy about the dumpy languor but 'witty, mature' . . . what better false impression could one want to give? Robert Robinson came down from the *Sunday Times* and thought the whole thing most stylishly done: 'It lent authenticity to the current Oxford maxim that it is smart to act.'

One long vac we toured Germany with *St Joan* and a damp verse play by Christopher Hassall. Among my fellow actors an editor of the *Spectator* (now an MP), the editor of *The Good Food Guide* and the editor of the *New Statesman* later emerged. In St Peter's-in-the-East, for the Poetry Society, one of my fellow Women of Canterbury was Maggie Smith. Smartest of all was the masque we did for Princess Margaret, *Porci ante Margaritam*, Swine before the Pearl, produced by Ned Sherrin in a panama hat.

Angus Wilson deplores the young who use their time at Oxford to further their careers in the outside world. Would that dashing blond, Michael Heseltine, have become Mr Heath's Minister for Aerospace and Shipping if he had not been President of the Union? It certainly can't have hindered him. My own careerism was purely Oxford-centred. In the outside world my ambition was limited (I wanted to work in a bookshop and learn to write). But the world was very interested in Oxford. *Encounter* and the *London Magazine* both began while I was up, and Stephen Spender and John Lehmann did a lot to encourage undergraduate contributors. The *Spectator* carried regular undergraduate articles. The poets were published in the weeklies as well as the little magazines. Revue sketches were transplanted to the West End. John Wood, whose splendid OUDS *Richard III* I remember, recalls it resulted not only in glowing reviews in the national press, but also in contract offers from the Old Vic, the Stratford Memorial Theatre, H. M. Tennant and Twentieth Century Fox! The careerists we resented were the undergraduate stringers who eagerly telephoned through to London every crumb of university scandal.

In those days, no women could dine in a man's college. One of our group, now Felicity Taylor, successfully challenged this blanket ruling when she dined as Jeremy Rundall's guest in

Lincoln—disguised improbably as a French boy. The college servants apparently did no more than raise a querying eyebrow. But the story leaked. Someone with his eyes on a Fleet Street career phoned the *Daily Express*. Cowley Place was thronged with reporters and St Hilda's felt obliged to rusticate Felicity until the end of term. Such an innocent prank nowadays would hardly merit a paragraph in the *Oxford Mail*.

'So the fun went on,' as Lord Boothby's did thirty years before. But it was not all fun and games. We thought a great deal about war and peace and the H bomb. Many of the men had already done their National Service. The Korean war ended in my first summer term. My brother had fought there; it had come very close to me. Our *Isis* was full of worried editorials and articles about whether the bomb should be banned or not: these were the first stirrings of what was later to be called CND. Then there was work. We certainly worked enough (often in the middle of the night) to justify our precious places. '*Paradise Lost* is the most marvellous stuff,' I enthused the day after dashing up to London for the Coronation. I think it was the only time I left Oxford in term time. I could hardly bear to be more than a mile or two from Carfax. I never went to Blenheim or even Boar's Hill. I rarely went further afield than the highest boat-house on the Cherwell or the Eynsham home of the Mellors, who ran the Fantasy Press. (Was that our Garsington?) A few weeks later I wrote: 'I forget much too frequently how much pleasure there is to be found in work.'

By the time, two years later, that I left Oxford I had stopped forgetting. This underlines the fact that not only is every single person's Oxford wholly individual but each person's Oxford is different from year to year, and indeed from term to term. I was ready to leave when the time came, to get married and go to Japan. I certainly did not feel, as Lord Boothby did, that I should never be so happy again. But Oxford had meant a great deal to me. I can understand Harold Nicolson's remark about the name on the jar of marmalade.

ANN THWAITE

Lord Boothby

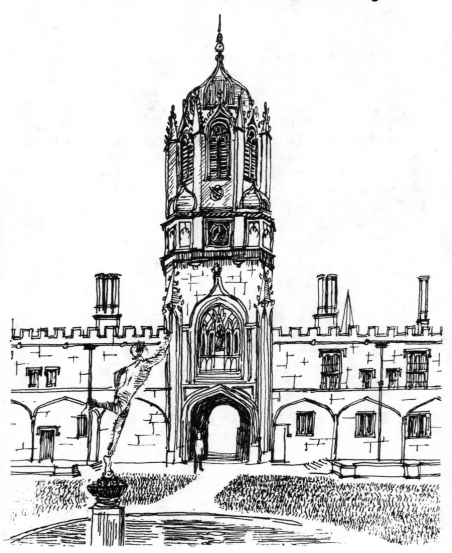

Robert Boothby was knighted in 1953 and made a life peer as Baron Boothby, of Buchan and Rattray Head, in 1958. He was born in 1900 and educated at Eton and Magdalen College, where he took his B.A. in 1921. He was Unionist MP for East Aberdeenshire from 1924 to 1958. He was at one time Parliamentary Private Secretary to Winston Churchill, and Parliamentary Secretary to the Ministry of Food. He has been Rector of St Andrews University, Chairman of the Royal Philharmonic Orchestra and President of the Anglo-Israel Association, and has done a great deal of broadcasting. He has been married twice.

J was commissioned in the Scots Guards on or about Armistice Day, November 11, 1918. Soon afterwards I was sent for by the Colonel of the Regiment, at his headquarters in Wellington Barracks. He said: 'You have passed well out of the Household Brigade Officer Cadet Battalion, and we have a good report about you from Captain Oliver Leese. I have now received orders to offer you a permanent commission in the Regiment. Alternatively, you are to be demobilized the day after tomorrow. I am sorry that you have only twenty-four hours to decide your future career, but that is how things are these days.'

'What am I to do?' I asked.

'Go away and think,' he said, 'and come back tomorrow morning with your decision.'

I had no one to consult. I spent a sleepless night. Then I went back and told the Colonel that I wanted to be demobilized, and to go up to Oxford. After all, had we not just fought 'the war to end all wars'? There seemed, at that moment, to be no future in the army.

I chose Magdalen (it was a happy choice), and sat for my college examination early in 1919. Somewhat to my surprise, for my Latin was very rusty, I got through, and shared digs for the summer term with my old friend Roger Senhouse, who had been with me at Eton and Bushey (the Guards' equivalent

of Sandhurst), and was also at Magdalen. I bought a motor
bicycle called a Radco, and settled down to enjoy myself.

Oxford after the First World War was a strange place. Not
many of the undergraduates who had been there before the
war came back. Nearly all of them had been killed. And most
of the few who survived understandably could not face returning to Oxford. There were no 'freshmen'. We were all equal. And
our job was nothing less than to re-create the university. On
the whole we succeeded. For example, someone remarked one
day that before the war there had been a thing called the
Gridiron Club, where the food and the company were good.
We formed a small committee, and started it up again at the
top of the High. It was a tremendous success.

In the summer vacation I went, with my three closest friends,
Roger Senhouse, Michael Llewelyn-Davies, and Clive Burt,
to a 'pension' at Saint-Servan in Brittany, owned and run by
Madame Baron, whom I reduced to helpless laughter whenever
I tried to talk French, which I frequently did. Roger was an
eccentric, with infinite charm. He was no soldier. We shared a
tent at Bushey, and one day the whole Company was marched
through it to see how a tent should not be left. He was never
really happy until he went to Bloomsbury and there, amongst
the writers, developed his own literary flair, and became a
successful publisher. Lytton Strachey, who loved him, left him
his library. Roger's rooms were always a shambles: priceless
books scattered all over the floor and two deep on the shelves.
But he knew exactly where they all were; and, as Jeffery
Amherst has told us in his autobiography, never failed to find
a bottle of gin, though sometimes only after a prolonged search.
When I got into political difficulties in 1940 because of an
allegation that I had failed to declare a personal interest when
advocating the repayment of Czech assets in this country to
their owners, and had to defend myself in the House of
Commons, it was Roger who came to my flat and took me there.
Afterwards I said to him: 'I have helped to enable thousands
of Czech refugees to start a new life in freedom; and it is the

best thing I have done in politics.' He replied: 'You are right.' We went back to the flat, where we found John Strachey. And there we drank a toast—to myself, and to Magdalen.

Michael was one of the five Llewelyn-Davies boys whom J. M. Barrie ran into in Kensington Gardens one day, and by whom he was immediately captivated. Their father was an impoverished barrister, their mother a daughter of George du Maurier and sister of Gerald. Without any legal fuss Barrie took them all over, sent four of them to Eton, and one into the Navy. I used quite often to go and talk to Michael in Adelphi Terrace and sometimes, after about half-an-hour, a tiny figure with black hair and glowing eyes would crawl out of the deep recesses of the enormous fire-place. It was Barrie.

Michael was the only one of my contemporaries at Oxford who seemed to me to be touched by genius. There was nothing he could not do, with effortless ease, except swim. I can still see his face disappearing beneath the waters of the river Rance, where we used to bathe, while Roger tried to hold him up. Barrie said that one day the flags of his college would fly for him; but I could find in him no trace of worldly ambition. '*You* can be a success, if you want to be,' he once said to me, 'provided we can keep you on the rails.' His own genius was purely creative. Apart from an intense admiration for Mr Lloyd George, he was uninterested in politics. Lady Violet Bonham-Carter, who heard of him, tried to get in touch with him. 'Who is this Mrs Carter?' he said to me indignantly. 'What does she want with me?' I think he might have become an artist like his grand-father (he was brilliant in pen and ink), or a writer like his cousin Daphne du Maurier, or both. That he would have done something pretty great I have no doubt. Instead he was drowned at a weir near Oxford, on a lovely summer afternoon. It profoundly affected the lives of his friends, certainly my own. I have a notion that Edward Marjoribanks, the brilliant half-brother of Quintin Hailsham, who wrote me a desperate letter, would never have taken his life if Michael had been alive.

As for Barrie, the fires of a grief to which I know no parallel scorched all the dross away, and drove him to the peak of his achievement—his Rectorial Address on Courage at St. Andrews University. After that he did nothing more.

Clive Burt got everything at Eton, where he was a scholar. Every colour, every prize. Success never went to his head. By nature he was sunny, gay and modest. Everyone loved him. When he left Eton he was, without question, the star of the school. At Oxford he had many friends—I was, I think, the closest; but his career was undistinguished. It was the same when he went on to the Bar where he was popular but never went very far. Gradually he faded. This was perhaps inevitable. If you reach the heights at Eton (I myself reached the bottom), you are bound to feel that life has no further achievements to offer which are worth having. I have seen it happen so often. Indeed, I can think of only two exceptions to the rule, Alec Douglas-Home and Hugh Kindersley.

While we were at Saint-Servan, we used to walk or take a tram to Saint-Malo, only a mile or two away, almost every evening. There we sat outside a café, and drank green chartreuse, and talked as only undergraduates can talk. We also found a casino with 'Boule'. It was my first introduction to gambling. We played nervously and cautiously with five-franc pieces; and I shall never forget Michael's delight when he won. Then we went to Paris for the Peace Procession. At evening, when we got there, the Champs Elysées was already crowded. We climbed a tree, and sat there all night. At ten o'clock next morning the procession began, headed by the three French Marshals, Foch, Joffre and Pétain, riding alone. After that it was poilus, in their blue uniforms, all the way. Haig, with his five Army Commanders, rode by in a single line. They were hardly noticed. The crowd kept on shouting: 'Vive les poilus!' Then, at last, a company of the Scots Guards appeared. Together we shouted 'Vive Bradshaw!' to the stalwart officer in command. He heard, and looked up, startled. We had a marvellous dinner that night, and then sadly broke up.

I went back for the autumn term to find that I had been given rooms in college. My 'scout', Messenger, was first class. The chef at Magdalen, a plump man with a beaming pink face, was the best I have ever come across in my whole life. Pre-war prices prevailed. We drank hock from the Emperor of Austria's cellars at seven shillings and sixpence a bottle. The life of the college hinged round Gynes, who had an office under the Junior Common Room where he dispensed a variety of good things to eat and drink, and also good advice. He might have been a millionaire. He was a great friend of William Morris, later Lord Nuffield, who kept a bicycle shop in Holywell before the war, and asked him to join him. I am sure that he had a happier life running Magdalen.

I had decided to read History. I took the shortened war course, which meant that you took three subjects out of five, and were not classed. You either got an Honours Degree, or you failed. I was warned that the standard was pretty high. I went to Grant Robertson's lectures, which I greatly enjoyed, but otherwise didn't do much work. I soon found that there were far too many other things to do. As I had rowed at Eton, I took up rowing at Magdalen, where we had two blues in the Oxford Eight, Sebastian Earl and A. T. Durand. For a time I stroked the Second Eight. Then Earl said to me, with truth: 'You are not pulling your weight.' He took me out in a dinghy, and we rowed together. 'Keep the boat straight,' he shouted to the cox whose name, if I remember right, was Hoskins. 'I can't,' came the reply. 'He's pulling you round.' I much enjoyed this, but came to the conclusion that the whole thing was far too strenuous for me, and gave it up. This was a disappointment for my cousin R. C. Bourne who, before the war, had stroked Oxford four times to victory.

I turned to golf. Here I was at a disadvantage because I had an inferiority complex. My father's handicap was plus two, and I never came within sight of beating him. Hopefully Roger Wethered asked me to play in the trials for the Oxford team at Frilford. I lost my nerve, and played worse than usual. I then decided that the best thing to do about golf was to enjoy it, and this I did. In those days amateur golf in Britain was dominated by two giants, Roger Wethered and Cyril Tolley; and I was fortunate enough to be a friend of both. In 1921 my father was Captain of the Royal and Ancient Golf Club of St Andrews. When the Open Championship was played there I went up to see it. I walked round with Roger, who had not yet been heard of. To begin with we were alone together, with a dog. It was a windless day. 'Talk to me about anything except golf,' he said. So I remained silent as I watched him put the ball on five successive greens round the turn—an almost unparalleled feat—and hole out in three at each. He would have won the championship if he hadn't accidentally trodden on his ball when he went to look at a line to the green. As it was he tied, and lost the play-off to Jock Hutchinson. Cyril Tolley later won the Amateur Championship at Muirfield.

Life in college was almost unbelievably good. We usually lunched in our rooms, and dined in hall, off superlative food and drink. John Strachey, then a high Tory, was there. We became Joint Editors of the *Oxford Review*. Lord David Cecil was Literary Editor, and Eddie Sackville-West Musical Editor; and we published William Gerhardi's first short story. Gerald Gardiner was also there. Though his academic career was undistinguished, he made his mark as a strong personality. He had great charm, and was an extremely good actor. He devoted most of his time to the Oxford University Dramatic Society, and I am quite sure that, if he had gone on the stage, he would have got to the very top. He chose instead to become one of England's leading counsel, and ultimately Lord Chancellor. Others I knew well were Gladwyn Jebb, who was extremely good-looking, and also good at games, but rather aloof; Kyrle Leng, a son of the famous Dundee newspaper proprietor; and Guy Warrack, our musician. Then, suddenly, Compton Mackenzie burst upon the scene, and overwhelmed us all. Here was a dazzling figure, still at the height of his powers and fame.

It is difficult to describe the spell he cast. I have known only three other men who have equalled him in this respect—Lloyd George, Birkenhead and Beecham. Like them he was marvellous company, and dominated any company in which he found himself. He had been at Magdalen, and adored it. One evening he came to dinner with me, and afterwards we punted, with two or three friends, down the river. I couldn't punt. As we went round in circles, bumping into a moored punt first on one bank then on the other, he laughed so much that he nearly fell into the water. Thus began a lifelong friendship which I have perhaps valued more than any other.

Guy Warrack said I should take my voice seriously, and it was through him that I met Freddie Grisewood, who was teaching singing in the university. He told me that I had the makings of a very good baritone voice, and asked me whether I wanted to be a singer. I said I thought I wanted to be a politician. 'You can't be a politician *and* a singer,' he said, 'but I can teach you something that may be of use to you—voice production. How to breathe, and how to pitch your voice.' He did, and it has stood me in good stead ever since. Freddie went on to make a career all his own in broadcasting.

Then I turned to politics. At that time there were only two undergraduates whose names commanded public attention—Leslie Hore-Belisha and Beverley Nichols. Both became President of the Union. Both were extraordinarily good speakers—Beverley, if anything, the better of the two. Neither fulfilled his early promise. Belisha was a strange man: highly intelligent, but hardly able to do anything for himself. All memoranda, despatches and letters had to be read aloud to him. Even his boots had to be laced up. He brought Liddell Hart, too late, to the War Office; but the Generals hated him. Shortly before he was sacked as Secretary of State for War, he asked me to dine with him alone. He told me that he was very worried about the position in France. His reasons were cogent, and his fears were soon proved to be fully justified. Towards the end of his life he spent much of his time in a monastery. He will be remembered for beacons, which he introduced when he was Minister of Transport.

Beverley was too gentle for politics. I no longer think, as once I did, that he could have stood the roughness of political life. He became a highly competent journalist, but he did not make as much money as Godfrey Winn did, under the guidance of Maugham. Anthony Eden was unknown. He was a recluse, with a small circle of friends who called themselves the Dilettante Society. He played no part in university politics, but he got a First in Oriental Languages.

Edward Marjoribanks introduced me to politics when he invited me to read a paper to the Canning Club, the most select Tory Club in the university, which met in different colleges at regular intervals to the accompaniment of an enormous punch-bowl, which belonged to the club, filled with mulled claret. I had the audacity to choose as my subject 'The Conduct of Naval Operations during the War of 1914–18.' My home in Scotland was near Rosyth and, as a boy, thanks largely to the kindness of Admiral Arthur Leveson, I had seen a lot of the Grand Fleet. I got away with it, and was later elected Secretary of the Canning Club. This enabled me to meet some of the leading statesmen of the day. Soon afterwards Churchill (Colonial Secretary) and Birkenhead (Lord Chancellor) came down to speak at the Union. Victor Cazalet gave a small party for them in his rooms at Christ Church, to which I was invited. Churchill was in full spate, and harangued us all for about twenty minutes. Suddenly he paused for breath. In the ensuing silence Lord Birkenhead, who was sitting in a corner, said in sibilant tones:' Shut up, Winston. It's not as if you had a pretty voice.' Churchill remained silent for the rest of the evening. I think that Birkenhead was his only friend on absolutely level terms. Churchill was rather frightened of him. In his account of Birkenhead in *Great Contemporaries*, he wrote: 'People were afraid of him and of what he would say. Even I, who knew him so well, refrained from pushing ding-dong talk too far when others were present lest friendship should be endangered.'

Lord Birkenhead was perhaps at his best with under- graduates. He always made us feel not only that he preferred our company to any other, but that he was himself still an undergraduate. He came often to Oxford. One day he arrived with a straw hat on the back of his head, and a large pink carnation in his buttonhole, looking about thirty-five. He told me that when he had asked for a glass of beer at Paddington Station at ten o'clock in the morning, the barmaid had called him a saucy boy. 'I suppose,' he said, 'that it is the first time the Lord Chancellor of England has been called a saucy boy.' I said that it was one of his greatest achievements. On another occasion, when he was prevented from dining with the Canning Club by an unexpected summons to the Peace Conference in Paris, he offered to come to breakfast instead. I viewed this proposal with some misgiving; and my apprehensions seemed to be fully justified when he arrived and sat in sombre silence for several minutes. Finally, he turned to me with a visible effort and said: 'Except for one melancholy occasion at Ten Downing Street, this is the first time I have breakfasted in company for twenty years; and I hope to God it is the last.' I ordered a tankard of draught cider, which revived him, and he made the usual brilliant impromptu speech. I owe my friend- ship with Lord Birkenhead entirely to Oxford. Later on, when I became a Member of Parliament, I always consulted him when I was in difficulty with my Party, and invariably got good advice. He once said to me, prophetically: 'You will always be in and out of trouble; but if you stick to your con- stituency, and they stick to you, no one will ever be able to break you.' Shortly before he died I asked him what he really thought of Lloyd George. He replied, laconically: 'I have not yet discerned his equal.'

I never stood for office in the Union; but I spoke there pretty frequently. My college, which was rather snobbish, did not approve of this; but I persisted. In 1922 Austen Chamberlain, the Leader of the Conservative Party, came down to a dinner given jointly by the Canning and Chatham Clubs and made what was, for him, an impassioned speech in favour of the continuation of the Coalition Government. We all agreed with him. Unfortunately the meeting of Conservative MPs at the Carlton Club in the autumn took a different view. They got rid of Lloyd George, Chamberlain, Churchill, Balfour, Birkenhead, and Horne in a single afternoon. The decline and fall of the British Empire then began. It did not take long.

So much for politics. The dons under whose influence I fell were 'Sligger' Urquhart, the Dean of Balliol; R. H. Dundas, a distant relative of mine, who was Senior Censor at Christ Church; A. T. Carter, tutor in Law at Christ Church; and L. B. Namier, tutor in History at Balliol. Urquhart's influence was the widest, and extended far beyond his own college. The reason for this was, I think, a simple one. He genuinely liked the young, he was the kindest man I have ever known, and he was always out to help. He had a chalet above Saint-Gervais in Haute Savoie, where he used to invite a certain number of undergraduates for reading parties during the summer vacation. He asked me to go there, and I did. The climb to the chalet from the railway station was long and stiff, and when you got there the life was pretty spartan. Simple food, white wine in moderation, mountain walks and work were the order of the day. He then arranged for a few of us to walk round, and finally to climb, Mont Blanc. Among the party were two great friends of mine, Peter Rodd and Charles Mathew. At that time all three of us were wild. Sligger put me in charge, and gave me the necessary money. All went well until we got to Courmayeur. There Peter found a casino, and that was the end of the money. After that we lived on tick. I didn't much like climbing Mont Blanc. But the hut where we slept near the summit was extremely comfortable, and the view next morning magnificent. Then we came down the Mer de Glace very fast. So fast indeed that the Swiss guide, who should have roped us, couldn't keep up and was sick. We were told afterwards that to jump the crevasses unroped, as we did, was extremely dangerous. Fortunately we did not know it. At Chamonix we had the first good meal and the first bath for several days. I then decided that it was better to look at mountains and glaciers from the bottom rather than the top, and have stuck to this ever since.

Peter Rodd was an infant prodigy. He looked sixteen, was a perfect linguist, and talked non-stop. This didn't matter because, if you were bored, there was no need to listen. Once, when he was talking to me about the Tuareg tribes of North Africa, he paused and said: 'You are paying no attention.'

'Not the faintest,' I replied; and he went on about the Tuaregs.

He had great qualities. He was loyal, affectionate, sympathetic and brave. He also had an extremely good, if rather disorganized brain. A remarkable career was predicted for him. It did not happen. I was his best man when he married Nancy Mitford. The marriage fell to pieces, as indeed did everything he touched. But she remained very fond of him to the end. So did his friends. Nobody who knew him well could help being fond of him. Some of us hoped that he might find scope for his undoubted talents, and also himself, in war. He didn't. His friend Basil Murray, the son of Gilbert Murray, who was also gifted but not, I think, a very good influence, went the same way to nowhere. Their only claim to fame is to have provided material for Evelyn Waugh, who made good use of them both in his novels.

After Oxford I did not see Charles Mathew for thirty years, until I went on a Parliamentary Delegation to the Far East. I sat next to him at a dinner in Kuala Lumpur given by the High Commissioner and found, to my astonishment, that he was Chief Justice of Malaya. He was quite unchanged, and greeted me as if we were still at Sligger's chalet.

'Is it fun?' I asked.

'That is not a question,' he replied, 'that is usually put to a Chief Justice, but I am enjoying myself.'

Robin Dundas was, from all accounts, a good scholar and an excellent tutor. He was apt to ask undergraduates rather intimate questions about their private lives. A few found it embarrassing, most were relieved to unburden themselves. I enjoyed it enormously, and invented answers which I thought would please him. He spoke and wrote in short brief sentences, always to the point. His postcards (he seldom wrote a letter), always signed D, were written in a clear but minute script. He told Maurice Bowra that he was, at heart, 'a motherly soul'. And so he was. He asked me often to dine with him at High Table in Christ Church. There I met F. A. Lindemann, later to become Lord Cherwell, and Churchill's closest adviser before and during the war. We took an instant dislike to each other, which the passage of time did nothing to diminish. Churchill knew of this, and later took good care to see that we never met. I regretted his influence over Churchill only because, in addition to his Germanic ruthlessness, I thought he was nearly always wrong.

'Don' Carter, as he was called, another of the dons who influenced me, was the antithesis of Urquhart: a bon viveur, completely cynical, with a rich sardonic sense of humour. I used to lunch with him, on occasion, in his rooms at Christ Church. He had very good taste: beautiful furniture, a magnificent collection of old silver, and an excellent cellar. His food and drink were superb; and his anecdotes, not always kind, were accompanied by a chuckle which I can hear to this day. He told me that long ago, before the turn of the century, he had asked one of my father's sisters to marry him. I asked my aunt if this was true, and she said it was. 'I was tempted,' she said, 'because he was such good company. But I couldn't marry him because he had eyes like a snail.' He was a great friend of Birkenhead, who admired his mind with professional legal appreciation, and made him a King's Counsel.

So the fun went on. I have never enjoyed myself so much. Two other close friends of mine were Cyril Radcliffe and Maurice Bowra. They were certainly the most successful. Under

Wilfrid Greene, Cyril was soon acknowledged to be one of our greatest lawyers and, at an early age, was promoted straight from the Bar to the House of Lords. During the war, as Director-General of the Ministry of Information, he established, with Brendan Bracken, the best relationship between a Minister and the Permanent Head of his Department that I have ever seen. After the war two of his colleagues told me that, as a Law Lord, he might have shaped our common law in a decisive fashion and in the tradition of some of his greatest predecessors, if he had wished to do so. He preferred to become chairman of a number of royal commissions and public enquiries, some of whose reports have made history.

A good deal of nonsense has been written about Maurice Bowra by people who did not know him half as well as I did. He was quite uncomplicated; he was a complete extrovert; and he had a marvellous capacity for putting undergraduates, especially shy ones, at their ease, and then for bringing them out. He was disappointed when Gilbert Murray did not recommend him for the Regius Professorship of Greek. But he was far better placed as Warden of Wadham, where he made his name and fame. I think he was also disappointed when he wasn't asked to do anything in the war, for he was a great administrator as well as a great scholar. (Lindemann could have put this right, but didn't.) I was glad to be able to give both Bowra and Radcliffe the honorary degree of LL.D. when I became Rector of St Andrews. I think it pleased them. In proposing the toast of the university at the Rectorial Dinner, Cyril made the best speech I have ever heard—and I have heard a lot.

Then there was Peter Ralli. He came up to New College with what was then a small fortune, and spent almost all of it on entertaining his friends. He looked, as Maurice Bowra said, like an old-fashioned Dutch doll. He gave delicious dinners in his candle-lit rooms in Holywell, with pink champagne. Some were for what he called aesthetes, and others for 'hearties'. Happily I was included in both. Maurice has described him as 'wonderfully perceptive and entertaining, and a most rewarding waster of time'. Among the hearties was Douglas Jardine. He was gentle and charming: but he regarded cricket not as a game but as war. When, as captain of the English Test team, he took Larwood out to kill the Australians, there was, as I predicted, quite a serious rift between the two countries. Peter never thought of work or games. When he took his History finals he answered, I think, only one question. It consisted of a single sentence, in his enormous handwriting: 'Her subjects wanted Queen Elizabeth to abolish tunnage and poundage, but the splendid creature stood firm.' When he came to London he spent the rest of his fortune on entertaining his friends at the Embassy Club, and then died. In his short life he had, again in Maurice's words, derived and given enormous pleasure.

I have read somewhere—I think in Montgomery Hyde's review of Christopher Hollis's book—that the new fashion in Oxford clothes was started by Harold Acton. This is not true. Harold was one of the generation which succeeded mine, and made his own impact. The new fashion was started by me, with the help of Hall Brothers in the High: brightly-coloured shirts without stripes, soon to be complemented by what became known as Oxford bags. As it was my sole creative achievement at the university, I must claim it.

One day I saw a ponderous solitary figure standing in the middle of Balliol quad. It beckoned to me, for Lewis Namier was not one to move unless it was necessary. When I reached him, he said: 'You have been living a life of pure pleasure. I am not against that. But you have done no work. I'm afraid you will not get your degree.'

'What can I do?' I asked.

'It is too late for reading and writing,' he said. Then he gave a deep sigh, and went on: 'There is now only one hope. Talking.'

'To whom?' I asked.

'To me,' he replied.

I went at once to see the President of Magdalen, Sir Herbert Warren, and told him that I wanted to go to Namier.

'On the face of it, this is a reflection on our History tutors,' he said. 'Fortunately for you, I was at Balliol myself, and Mr Jowett once told me that your grand-father was one of his favourite pupils.'

'He was my mother's god-father,' I interjected.

He beamed. 'Well,' he said, 'I would not let you go to any other college, but you can go to Namier. I think Jebb would like to accompany you. If so, I will let him.'

So Gladwyn and I went to Namier. It was one of the richest experiences of my life. With the possible exception of C. H. K. Marten, of Eton, he was the best teacher I have ever known. Our special subject was the French Revolution. He could bring the whole sweep of it into the compass of a single hour. 'You are bound to get a question about Danton,' he said. 'There are two views about Danton, one orthodox, the other unorthodox. I will give you both.' We got the question. I chose the unorthodox view, and I think this is what got me my degree. Anyway, thanks to Namier, I got it. I was asked to give the Address at his Memorial Service. I ended by saying: 'Of the man himself I would say only this. He gave affection, and needed it. He found it not only in the love of his wife, and of a close circle of friends, but in the deep admiration of a host of pupils now scattered all over the world; in greater measure, perhaps, than he himself ever realized.'

When I left Oxford for good, in 1922, I had a compartment in the train to myself; and sat alone, thinking. I came to the conclusion that, despite the stunning blow of Michael's death, I should never be so happy again. I was right. I never again escaped the influence that A. E. Housman had over all my generation.

> '*They say my verse is sad: no wonder;*
> *Its narrow measure spans*
> *Tears of eternity, and sorrow,*
> *Not mine, but man's.*

This is for all ill-treated fellows
  Unborn and unbegot,
For them to read when they're in trouble
  And I am not.'

Raymond Massey

Raymond Massey was born in Toronto in 1896. His brother was Vincent Massey, one-time Prime Minister of Canada. He was educated at school in Ontario, at Toronto University and at Balliol College (1919–1921). He has been awarded honorary degrees from seven different universities. He served as a lieutenant in the Canadian Field Artillery in France in 1916 and was wounded. In the Second World War he was on the staff of the Adjutant General of the Canadian Army. He became an American citizen in 1944. He first appeared on the professional stage in 1922 and has since appeared in hundreds of plays, films and television episodes. He co-starred as Dr Gillespie in the long-running television series 'Dr Kildare'. He has been married three times and two of his children are also well known on the stage.

In the Michaelmas term of 1919, I went up to Balliol College. At that time, Balliol was the undisputed intellectual focus of the university. I believe it remains so to this day. I never could understand why I was in such an environment, and the college and I did not really come to terms. I believe the fault was almost all mine, except that my brother was an enthusiastic Balliol man with persuasive powers.

Balliol is the second oldest college in Oxford University, founded in 1263 by a flourishing Norman noble named John de Balliol and Dervorguilla, his wife. During the following centuries, Balliol College was joined by some thirty-three later foundations. In 1870, the Fellows of Balliol College elected Benjamin Jowett, Doctor of Divinity, as Master. It was a significant appointment. Hitherto, the colleges of Oxford had proceeded on a more or less even tenor of academic quality. But the new Master had definite ideas about the future of Balliol. An owlish, shrill-voiced little man, Jowett was a rare combination of scholar and activist, not only a don renowned in his classical field and the definitive translator of Plato, but also a determined and practical Master whose obsession was to make Balliol the intellectual leader of the university.

This he succeeded in accomplishing by unashamedly recruiting the best brains from leading public schools. He had an uncanny ability in spotting not only intellect but character in the young and he had representatives or scouts everywhere. Everybody knew Jowett and he knew everybody. He was the outstanding academic figure of the Victorian age.

Within a generation of Jowett's death, Balliol had produced men pre-eminent in nearly every phase of English life: prime ministers, churchmen, cabinet members, judges, pro-consuls, ambassadors, leaders in letters and the arts and every manner of public life. The University Honours List each year sparkled with Firsts attained by the college. There was a fierce loyalty and pride deep-set in Balliol men, usually concealed in British reticence, but expressed with emotional extravagance by Hilaire Belloc, who went up in 1892 and so had had two years of 'The Jowler':

> *'Balliol made me, Balliol fed me,*
> *Whatever I had she gave me again;*
> *And the best of Balliol loved and led me,*
> *God be with you, Balliol men.'*

My brother, who had been up in 1912 and 1913, had filled me with Balliol lore. I must admit that I went up to the college with a feeling that perhaps I was misplaced. I never overcame this apprehension.

Oxford had been hard hit by the war. Two thousand and seven hundred Oxford men had been killed, an academic generation virtually wiped out. The university was generous in the extreme in the accommodation of ex-servicemen. We were excused all examinations but the final Honours Schools and even these, if we wished, we could take on a so-called shortened course. I could in six terms write for my degree. Jowett must have turned over in his grave.

During the year 1919, some hundred and seventy-five of us came up to Balliol, just out of the army or navy. Most of us were a few years older than the usual undergraduates; yet we faced with equanimity, even with pleasure, the restrictions that a wise and ancient institution saw fit to impose on us 'junior members of the university'. After all, it was rather cosy to be regarded as still youthful.

On my staircase was Frank Sandford, a commander in the Royal Navy, who had taken the first submarine through the Dardanelles minefields in 1915. In the Zeebrugge Raid in 1918, he had rescued the crew of the blockship commanded by his brother, who won the V.C. My next-door neighbour was Andrew Rothstein, lance corporal in the Royal Engineers, and later London correspondent of TASS and director of the Information Department of the Russian Trade Delegation in 1921–24. He informed me that in the coming revolution, I would be the first to be put up against a wall and shot. Rothstein was the first Communist I had ever met. He was indignant that I had visited Siberia with a military force intended to interfere with the revolution, and I lost no opportunity of goading him into a rage.

There were six of us occupying rooms in this staircase which looked out on St Giles. It was one of two seventeenth-century buildings in the inner quadrangle. With the exception of a small, fourteenth-century Gothic library, these two buildings were the only ones to escape a devastating renovation in the nineteenth century. The new dining hall and chapel of Balliol, built sometime about 1860, are examples of the Victorian style of which John Ruskin had been the supreme advocate. The chapel, with its horizontal stripes of dark and light brown stone, is particularly offensive.

Oxford conjures up pictures in most minds of oak-panelled rooms, glowing fireplaces, upholstered wicker chairs, pipe smoke and endless, enlightened talk. Such pictures are true but not totally.

There was in my time no inside plumbing at Balliol. In the late eighteenth century, the college had received the gift of some twenty-four water closets from a thoughtful and generous noblewoman, the Lady Elizabeth Perriam. These facilities were housed in a flat-roofed building known as The Perriam against the wall bordering Trinity College and at a minimum distance of one hundred yards from all the staircases. It is proper that all the inevitable graffiti inscribed on the walls of this Balliol structure have been in impeccable Greek or Latin verse.

It was gracious living but with chamber pots. Since my Oxford days, I have acquired a collection of chamber pots, ranging from cloisonné and Spode to the simplest china with ribald inscriptions. I possess some twenty-five of these treasures to remind me of Balliol.

The hardest-worked men I have ever encountered, with the exception of coal miners, were the college scouts, who had to carry huge ewers of hot and cold water up as many as four storeys for 'sitz' baths and then carry the waste down again. They had to serve the breakfasts and clear away the debris, clean the rooms, make the fires and quite often serve luncheons in the rooms of their young men.

The scout on my staircase, Number IV, was an old fellow named Bliss. He had been a scout at Balliol for over forty years. In the long summer vacations, he used to work as a waiter in a hotel at Lynton on the north Devon coast. I had met him when I was there with my family in the summer of 1912. He told me much about Balliol, where my brother had been the previous year. Bliss said that his work at Mr Hole's Cottage Hotel at Lynton was a perfect rest after serving six young gentlemen on staircase IV. I saw his point seven years later.

The high point of Bliss's career was serving the future Marquess of Curzon in 1878, when he was living in the rooms I later occupied in the college.

In my time, none of the occupants of Number IV staircase matched the elegance of Lord Curzon; but with the departure of Rothstein in my second year, the tone was considerably improved. He was replaced by my old school friend from Appleby, John Harlan, who came up to Balliol in 1920 as a Rhodes Scholar. This made the number of future lawyers four out of the six of us: Mr Justice Harlan of the US Supreme

Court; Lord Evershed, Lord Chief Justice of England; Mr
Justice Barry and Bertram Bevan-Petman of the Inner Temple.
The last, named 'B-P', had been in the Indian Cavalry six or
seven years. When I knew him at Balliol I was able to understand the gold standard perfectly. B-P's finances were entirely
based on an 18-carat gold cigarette case. All I remember now
about his involved but sound theory is that 'it has to be a very
good cigarette case'. I also recall that he sometimes pawned
the case. Such emergencies he referred to as 'recessions'.

Normally one spent the first two years living in college and
the rest in lodgings. But as most of us were up for a shortened
course of six terms, we remained in college all our time.

No resident of the college could leave it after nine in the
evening or re-enter after midnight. Huge wooden gates were
locked with enormous padlocks at 9 pm, the only entrance
being by a tiny postern gate. I was relieved of this restriction
by the generosity of a friend, Harcourt Johnstone, who be-
queathed me a large key to the rear postern gate in St Giles
when he was sent down in the Hilary term of 1920. I also had
a room looking out on St Giles and the Martyrs' Memorial. It
allowed ingress through a window from the top of a hansom
cab driven up on the pavement. Several hansoms were still
plying in Oxford largely for this purpose, I think. I myself
never used this means of entry, preferring the key. One night,
about 1 am, a tap on my window from a cabby's whip summoned
me to open it. Four merry friends were passed into my room,
where for several hours they continued a party they had just
left at Magdalen.

Lunch and tea could be served in one's rooms when requested
and it was a popular form of hospitality. Late in my first term,
I invited two friends from Worcester College to lunch. As I had
been entertained well at Worcester, I was anxious to prove that
you could have good food at 'that dreary hydro on the Broad,'
as Balliol was often referred to by other colleges. Bliss had set
the table and brought the wine up, a bottle of sherry and some

claret. I thought I would give my guests mulled claret, a popular drink in those days. I set a bottle on the trivet in front of a good hot fire.

No young bride ever fussed about her first meal for her in-laws more than I did for these guests of mine. I straightened the knives and forks, dusted the glasses over and over and finally came to rest standing with my back to the fire.

I was looking at my watch when the explosion took place. I had forgotten about the bottle coming to the boil on the trivet. Luckily, I was wearing a pair of heavy corduroy trousers and the glass didn't penetrate them. My guests and I picked up the fragments scattered all over the room.

Bliss brought up another bottle. 'Try it at room temperature, sir,' he said. 'Mr Curzon always did.'

Oxford learning was based on the tutorial system. Each scholar or commoner in the college was assigned to a tutor, perhaps to two or even more, in the 'school' for which he was reading. My school was Modern History, my tutor Kenneth Bell. He was not only a brilliant scholar but a remarkable human being, kindly, witty, humorous and understanding; we became close friends. He had lectured in Toronto University for three years and, during four years' service in the Royal Field Artillery, had won an M.C., been wounded and commanded a battery. Now he was back at Balliol as one of three History tutors. As Junior Dean of the college, he was in charge of the discipline.

Six or eight of us would go to Kenneth for tutorials twice a week and sometimes I would have a little extra time. These sessions were informal, no two of them alike. The aim of Kenneth Bell was not to impart knowledge but to make us think. History was to be approached in a legalistic, analytical manner. We had to speak up in those tutorials of his. If we were silent, it was evidence of not thinking and that was failure. I realized almost at once that my fellows in the tutorial were just plain better than I was, better prepared and more articulate. In my second term, I asked Kenneth point blank, 'I'm in fast company. Can I make the grade in Schools?'

'You're mentally lazy,' he answered directly. 'Possibly it's timidity. But Schools are not competitive and, as far as the college is concerned, we can do with a leavening of intellectual vagrancy.'

For the first two terms, I went to the Dean, Francis Fortescue Urquhart, once a week for another tutorial. He was known as 'Sligger' and his sessions were just as easy-going as Kenneth's. Sligger was a devout Roman Catholic who spent many of his vacations on a round of visits to the houses of recusant nobility. A good tutor, he dealt with the political philosophy of Modern History, which entailed the reading of such enchanting works as Hobbes's *Leviathan*, John Locke and John Stuart Mill. Even Sligger, who had a pretty wit, could not alleviate my boredom with Mill.

The Master kept tabs on us by requiring an occasional essay. I have one that I submitted in the Hilary term of my first year. It is entitled, 'The Separation of the Functions of Government is the Greatest Discovery of Political Science'. I have read it again after fifty years and I find it has not improved with age. I have this satisfaction: my essay must have bored the Master as much as a lecture of his on 'The Poor Laws in England in the Nineteenth Century' bored me. This was the only lecture I went to at Oxford. Attendance at lectures was voluntary and I found I could borrow the notes of friends and avoid the crush of eager women undergraduates who thronged these gatherings. Lectures were the only university activities in which the sexes met. I convinced myself that the written word was more compelling than the spoken; at least it was less liable to be mislaid.

The Master was a cobwebby little man with a high-pitched voice. His name was A. L. Smith. A formidable scholar, he was steeped in the tradition of maintaining Balliol's intellectual supremacy. Beyond a couple of ritualistic tea parties at the

Master's lodgings and the submission of my essay, I saw little of him until my last term.

A curious phenomenon of Balliol was the singing or moaning of a strange ditty called 'Gordooley' on every conceivable occasion, by any number of Balliol men, drunk or sober. It had a simple libretto of two lines and the tune was reminiscent of a mournful bugle call such as 'The Last Post'. The words were: 'Oh, Gordooley—got a face like a ha-a-am. . . . Bobby Johnson says so and he ought to know!' That's all there was to it. Who or what Gordooley was, nobody ever knew, except that apparently he was no rose to look at. As for Bobby Johnson, his identity is shrouded in mystery. For the previous hundred years, no member of the college had been so named. The chant was used nocturnally, as a rallying cry like an American college yell; or, in spite of its lugubrious, wailing tone, as an outburst of elation or just to annoy our next-door neighbours in Trinity College.

Since most of us undergraduates of the post-war years were older than the usual run of students, less 'youthful exuberance' might have been expected of us. In fact, we were as boisterous as previous generations. I remember two enthusiastic outbursts with pleasure.

The British government, in December, 1919, had distributed a vast number of captured German weapons as war trophies to cities, institutions and villages. Often these obnoxious relics were resented and consigned to the nearest pond or dump. Balliol was included in this governmental generosity. After the Christmas 'vac' that year, we found a large German minnenwerfer squatting in the centre of the Fellows' garden. It was an ugly contraption mounted on two wheels like a gun, weighing eight or nine hundred pounds; an unpleasant memento which, it was unanimously agreed, would have to go.

No plans were made. But a few nights after term began, there was, for no accountable reason, an unusual call for the doughty college ale in hall. Shortly afterwards, the sad strains of 'Gordooley' drifted from the Fellows' garden like a tocsin.

Gowned scholars and commoners swarmed to the ramparts. No orders were given. It was the will of us all that this metallic insult should be passed over the fifteen-foot wall into the gardens of Trinity. Where there's a will there's no weight; in a few minutes, the damned thing was on the roof of The Perriam, all eight hundred pounds of it.

There was now only about six feet of wall to carry. Trinity was offering some resistance, flowerpots coming over in a kind of barrage. But we were close to success now and twelve of us managed to get a hold. With a shout of 'Look out below, Trinity!' over it went. There was a crash of breaking glass as a cucumber frame in the Trinity president's vegetable garden perished.

The operation closed with three triumphant 'Gordooleys' and the happy discovery that Kenneth Bell, the Junior Dean, had joined the group on the Perriam roof, which had given the final heave. There had been no police brutality and academic freedom had been preserved.

In the next term, the university was visited by Princess Mary, the Princess Royal, who honoured Balliol by planting a tree in the Fellows' garden where the Hun mortar had been. The whole college witnessed the little ceremony and HRH was heartily applauded.

That night after hall, the Communists and radicals of the college, about fifteen of them, tried to dig the tree up. They were driven off with light casualties by a small band of royalists and conservatives. A picket was left to protect the tree.

About an hour later, the attack was renewed, both sides having been reinforced, and in this engagement, the tree suffered some injury. The attackers were again driven off and the tree was placed in protective custody in my rooms. It was replanted with splints applied to its fractured trunk by a small party of conservationists early the following morning.

This highly successful exercise in political science had an unfortunate culmination. The Junior Dean, who had performed so commendably in the affair of the German mine-thrower, appeared in his academicals and gated us for a week for interfering with college property. This decision resulted in the confinement to college at night of five loyal monarchists, including two future High Court judges. But, even if somewhat scathed, the Princess's tree survived.

The day I came up to Balliol, I became a rowing man, and in my six terms I never missed a day on the river. Those early autumn days were lovely and relaxing, and I thought how wise I had been to have chosen to row instead of wallowing about a rugger field in the muddy grass.

Rowing was more than a sport at Oxford, it was a cult. It was ingrained in the university, a great deal of the coaching being in the hands of dons. My first days of 'tubbing' in a heavy clapboard, four-oared contraption with fixed seats were directed by an antique don who apparently had come out of the woodwork. He wore a frayed, faded Leander cap, which meant he must have been an old Blue, a trials man or have rowed in a Head of the River boat. The Leander Club is exclusively restricted to such heroes of Oxford and Cambridge. His instruction was, I gathered, faithful to the orthodoxy of Oxford and Cambridge rowing, as developed at Eton, which has always supplied the universities with good oarsmen. Rowing, he explained, was an art in which the oar was moved through the water by the legs and the swing of the back: the arms were merely the connection of the back with the oar. This made the 'English' method of rowing a rhythmic movement of beauty.

He warned us that there was in being, in actual practice, a deplorable heresy preached by a man named Steve Fairbairn, an Australian, in which the back was disregarded in its proper emphasis and the arms were used to finish the stroke. This Australian had taught his baleful ideas to the crews of Jesus College, Cambridge, with the sad result that Jesus had gone Head of the River on the Cam before the war. Fairbairn had also taught the Jesus style to the Light Blue or Cambridge Eight with disgustingly successful results. He had even imparted his revolutionary ideas to a tideway rowing club which had done depressingly well at Henley in 1914. Fairbairn was quoted by the old don as having said, 'It's better to go fast than look good!' The blasphemy was whispered to us.

With due reverence for tradition and style, a very sore behind from the fixed thwart or seat on which we slid in those horrible heavy fours, and a savage determination to excel as a galley slave, I was weaned from the tubbing.

I was lucky enough to be in the winning four in some time tests and in the last week of term was picked as number three in the second Torpid for the bumping races in the Hilary term.

The winter had set in; it was late November and a time to try our souls. The Torpid boat was a heavy barge-like vessel with the same agonizing fixed seats as the four. We never missed a day at the Balliol Boat Club. Sometimes with chapped hands, ice in our hair and blood-stained shorts, we would return from an hour's workout and try to thaw ourselves around the tiny stove in the barge.

After the Christmas vac, Kenneth Bell took over the coaching of the second Torpid, or 'togger'. In the dictionary, torpid is said to mean lacking in energy, vim or vigour. Some Victorian don with a sick sense of humour must have given the winter term races the name. It was not appropriate for us. Though we may have lacked style, we certainly possessed vim and vigour.

When Trinity term started, I found to my astonishment that I had been picked as three in the college first Eight, which I held down for the Eights Week races. We rowed in a new *Lady Dervorguilla* shell with sliding seats, and my days of pain were over. With two Blues and several old Etonians in the boat, we weren't too bad. The college started the week in third place with Christ Church and Magdalen ahead of us. That's the way we finished.

Magdalen, with four Blues in her eight, went Head of the

River by bumping 'the House' opposite the Christ Church barge on Monday and Balliol rowed through every night—the word 'night' was always used instead of day in reference to both Torpids and Eights Week. We did gain on the House (so-called because of its Latin name 'Aedes Christi') by half a length almost every one of the five nights but couldn't pull off a bump.

Eights Week was a lovely sight that year. The weather was perfect and every day the barges filled with pretty women in bright summer frocks. The towpath opposite was a contrast with howling mobs following each boat, and signal pistol shots and shouts of 'You're going up, Merton,' 'It's a canvas, Trinity!' And of course, 'Well rowed, Balliol, well rowed!'

After Eights Week in 1920, the University Boat Club persuaded six colleges to send their First Eights to Henley Regatta. Oxford was making a determined effort to swamp the expected Cambridge invasion. Magdalen, Christ Church, Trinity, Exeter, Merton and Balliol were set to go, and Oxford had entries in every event in the Regatta. We were to row in the Ladies Plate, a race for colleges and public schools. The captain of the Balliol Boat Club was an Australian Rhodes Scholar named Hugh Cairns. A Blue, he had rowed in the Oxford boat the previous March and had rowed at seven in the college eight. He took himself out of the boat in order to coach us. We still had one Blue, Stanley O'Neil, at number six.

Hugh was a gentle, gregarious man, with many friends, among whom was Rudyard Kipling. Hugh brought him to our training table in hall one night before we left for Henley. Mr Kipling appeared much interested in rowing and our chances at Henley. After dinner, some of us adjourned to Kenneth Bell's rooms, Hugh and Mr Kipling along with us. It was a cheerful evening with much good talk, and Mr Kipling fitted in smoothly with the group.

A hero to us all, Kipling might have been just another don

as he curled up in a big chair with his mug of Balliol ale. He listened, talked a bit, laughed a lot and seemed to have a good time, whether he heard about the merits of swivel rowlocks, the virtues of the newest *Lady Dervorguilla*, the shell we were taking to Henley, or the usual small talk of training table. By the time we broke up, it had been arranged that Mr Kipling would accompany us to Henley. We had adopted him in a peremptory manner. He complied cheerily. Hugh Cairns said the house the college had rented for our two weeks at the Regatta would accommodate Mr Kipling in addition to the fourteen of us (Hugh was taking five substitutes as well as the eight).

Two days later, we made our first appearance on the river at Henley. There were thirty-five eights and twelve fours, to say nothing of pairs and sculls entered, and the course had to be reserved for time tests. All day long, one or another of the eights, fours, pairs and single scullers would be rowing a 'course', with a coach and followers with stop watches, all on bicycles, making the towpath as perilous to a casual pedestrian as Fifth Avenue or Piccadilly.

Mr Kipling was all attention, a stop watch concealed in his pocket, timing the crews who were rowing 'courses'. Since he could see starts from the Leander Club enclosure opposite the finishing post, he was able to time all our likely competition in the first two or three days. Nobody knew what he was doing. He was as furtive as a Newmarket clocker at early-morning gallops. He said the only other spy he detected was a bishop whose pink Leander cap clashed so violently with his purple bib that nobody in the enclosure could take their eyes off him. This chromatic disturbance fascinated Kipling. Greatly impressed with the influx of rowing clergy, he was convinced that a superb and stately crew composed entirely of bishops and deans, who were members of Leander, could be put on the river for a five-hundred-yard display.

After ten days at Henley, the Regatta opened with Balliol in fairly good shape. We won our first heat against the Royal

Military College by a length, but in the draw for the second day, we had been told the bad news. We were to row against Eton on Thursday. Although Eton was a public school, its crew was almost always better than the average college. This year was no exception. We faced an eight that had been superbly trained and was a good five pounds per man heavier than we were. Mr Kipling had timed them over a trial course at 7' 17", exactly their time in the heat against us. They won by a length. It was a galling defeat. We were rowed out. I couldn't breathe and held my head down between my knees. As we drifted under Henley Bridge, I remember a kindly cockney voice calling, 'Good old three—don't worry, you'll live!'

We paddled back to the boathouse and carried *Lady Dervorguilla* to her rack. Hugh Cairns and Mr Kipling appeared. They had watched the race from the umpire's launch and looked far from dejected.

'You rowed well, the best form you've showed,' Hugh told us. 'Now take it easy and about half-past seven tonight I'm going to put you over the course again, against the clock.'

We relaxed until about seven o'clock that night, then we took the shining shell out and paddled up to Temple Island. There we did some starts and short bursts of rowing. One of the substitutes got in the starting punt and steadied us for a start. Hugh called from the bank: 'I'll start you with a gun ... COME FORWARD . . ARE YOU READY? ... THE SHOT!' We were off. Arengo Jones, our stroke, set us about forty the first minute and then he settled down to what seemed about thirty-five. Something astonishing had happened. The boat was moving forward without our effort. As we came forward, she seemed to slide ahead of us. It was an extraordinary sensation of smooth movement. I felt I was slacking but I dared not press for we were, for the first time, completely together in a rhythmic cycle. Arengo was giving us great length and maintaining the rate of stroke. From the bank, Hugh Cairns on his bike shouted, 'Oh, well rowed, Balliol!'

We were passing the 1500-yard post. I could hardly believe we had come that far. Kimber, the cox, cried, 'Give her ten, Balliol!' and counted us through, Jones bringing us up to forty. We were nearly at Phyllis Court now. We could hear an orchestra playing. It was so easy. Good Lord, there's the enclosure on the Bucks side. Again Kimber shouted, 'Now row her in, Balliol, give her ten!' Ten good long ones we gave her, and it was over. 'Easy all, Balliol!'

From the bank by the Leander enclosure, now empty in the dusk, came Hugh's delighted words, 'Well rowed, Balliol, oh, well rowed!' Mr Kipling was shouting the time, but we couldn't hear him. We paddled back to the boathouse and, as we lifted the *Lady Dervorguilla* over our heads and placed her on the rack, Hugh, Mr Kipling and the substitutes came into the boathouse. We heard the good news that our time had been 7' 10"—three seconds better than Eton's in the morning. It was the best row I ever had, practically in the dark, racing against the clock, with no one to see us except Hugh Cairns and Rudyard Kipling.

In October, 1920, back at Oxford, I was in the thick of activity. The number of clubs, societies and organized groups within the university was prodigious. I belonged to the Raleigh Club, a collection of imperialists whose interests may be indicated by the toasts at the annual dinner in 1920—'The Empire of the Bretanes', 'The Dominions', 'India', 'The Crown Colonies'; and by the speakers, who included Lord Milner, Lord Meston and my brother Vincent, who had been president in 1913. All this was only sixty years ago, but there was not a sign of Tanzania, Volta, Ghana, Zambia or any of the newborn states that have replaced the Crown Colonies. The Empire was still a reality. South Africa was a staunch and loyal Dominion, of which Lord Milner had been the architect. Only over India was there a cloud in the sky and it was a little bigger than a loincloth. The war seemed to have made the

Empire more solid than ever, at least so it seemed to me after every meeting of the Raleigh Club.

The Brackenbury Society was an old and informal institution. It met periodically for discussion of some timely subject, often with a distinguished visitor. The club had about thirty members, most of whom attended meetings in the old Senior Common Room. At one meeting, T. E. Lawrence came to us. It was a disturbing occasion. I am always ill at ease in the presence of cold intellect. Sheer brain frightens me. Lawrence was bitter and brilliant. He had been allowed to make commitments and promises to the Arabs which were not kept by the British. But the sad fact is that in 1920, he foresaw exactly what is now happening in the Middle East. I have never forgotten that evening with an extraordinary man. We had the privilege of meeting other great men at 'Bracker' meetings: Lord Asquith, a Balliol prime·minister, was one of them, but there was never another like Lawrence.

As I joined every club, society, group or faction that would have me, except the Communist Party, I soon found myself a member of the Union. This was the university debating society. Its sessions were modelled closely on those of the House of Commons; and for more than a century, future statesmen, prime ministers and members had learned the ways of the House by debating motions, grave and frivolous, in the Union. The four principal speakers wore white tie and tails, as did the Speaker. A sergeant-at-arms was in attendance and sometimes he was not only ceremonial but necessary. Following the tradition of Westminster, all speeches were extemporaneous, even notes being unfavourably regarded.

Those were still the days of rhetoric and eloquence in public life: before the prepared statement and the speech-writer appeared, before the idiot cards and the teleprompter. The young men who spoke at the Union were worthy followers of Gladstone and Asquith. I remember Anthony Eden, who made quite a reputation for himself as a speaker in 1920 and 1921.

It was my misfortune to speak against a motion that had just received Eden's eloquent support. My friend from Balliol, the future writer Beverley Nichols, was in the chair as Speaker. As he 'recognized' me, there was a look of kindly pity on his face. With something approaching horror, I remember those minutes I stood in a crowded Union and tried to take Eden apart. The funny thing is, I haven't the foggiest recollection of what we were talking about. I spoke again several times but only after careful preparation; my attendance at the Union was primarily to hear my fellow members perform.

It is probably unfair to judge the Oxford University Dramatic Society by its activities in 1919–1920. The OUDS, in abeyance since 1914, had started up again after the war with an entirely new membership. I joined as soon as I could, and this was not so easy as it might have been. The society, which occupied some rather austere rooms in George Street, was run in the manner of a social club. Naturally I knew none of the members to propose and second me. The president, Maurice Colbourne, decided to waive such formalities in view of my obvious enthusiasm for the theatre. He exercised his presidential authority to make me a member forthwith. Other than myself, I think, he was the only member of the OUDS of that year of its revival who became a professional actor. He certainly was one of the few who gave performances of professional competence in the Society's first production.

The programme of the OUDS had never been ambitious: a few casual visits to the society's rooms by critics, managers, writers or actors, evenings of questions and mulled claret; the annual production in the Hilary term. I remember only Harley Granville-Barker coming for an evening's session, a great experience for me. It was my first encounter with a great professional theatre man. He was a Renaissance character— the actor, producer and playwright combined. As a playwright, he could write any kind of play from a farcical comedy like *Rococo* to *The Madras House*. As an actor, he couldn't help writing good dialogue.

It always puzzled me that Granville-Barker undertook the job of adapting or rather editing Thomas Hardy's *The Dynasts*. We played it at the New Theatre. John Drinkwater directed the production and about forty young gentlemen of the OUDS had speaking parts. I doubt if the best professional cast in the world could have handled Hardy's leaden verse. And we were amateurs. I played Caulaincourt in a brief scene of Napoleon's abdication before exile to Elba. I still remember my one speech. You don't forget a decisive defeat. I don't remember who played Napoleon. I had my own problem. It was deeply personal and I faced it in the best amateur tradition, without regard for my fellow performers. Eight times I spoke those deathless lines in front of an audience:

> '*We should have had success. But fate said no.*
> *And abdication, making no reserves,*
> *Is, sire, we are convinced, with all respect,*
> *The only road.*'

The choice of play was unfortunate. The war of a hundred years ago was not the most intriguing theatre fare for people who had lived through 1914–1918. The next year, the OUDS returned to the traditional Shakespearean production with a professional star in the leading feminine role. *The Dynasts* had been cast from the vast number of dons' daughters available for women's parts. In 1921, the committee selected *Antony and Cleopatra* with the beautiful Cathleen Nesbitt as Cleopatra. Cathleen afterwards married Cecil Ramage, who played Antony.

I dropped out of the OUDS during my second year and, with a college friend, Guy Vaughan-Morgan, organized a small play-reading club of fifteen members, mostly from Balliol. We met about every fortnight to read a play. We had about ten readings—plays by Ibsen, Galsworthy, Granville-Barker, Shakespeare, the usual selection of the eager and stage-struck. The 'performances' were sometimes quite effective in what was soon to become a radio technique. One thing is certain: we got more out of our nameless little group than the OUDS ever offered.

London was only an hour and a half away by train and matinees were possible without applying for leave. A night away from college was a different matter. All colleges were stern about such leaves. James Morris's excellent book, *Oxford*, tells of an undergraduate applying for an absence to attend the funeral of his uncle. The reply of the dean of the college was, 'Oh, very well . . . but I wish it could have been a nearer relative.'

Sometimes I am inclined to ridicule the caricatures of Victorian male attire which many of the young and would-be young of today have adopted, particularly for evening wear. But I curb my taunts when I think of my own garb when I went down to London for a day or an evening in '20 and '21. I had two suits, both pin-striped, a dark grey and a brown. White spats or a pair of grey-topped, black-buttoned boots always called for an agonizing decision. Light-coloured waistcoats and broad, striped club ties were in order, and good loud shirts. The ensemble was not in the least conspicuous at that time, nor did it lead my fellow passengers in the third-class carriage to expect that I would shortly produce a deck of cards.

Like a great many undergraduates, I was soon caught in the web of credit. Booksellers, shirtmakers, bootmakers, tailors, even the college stores, flaunted credit at you. In my first term, a Mr Stratton called at my rooms with a bag of cloth samples, a measuring tape and an agreeable personality. I ordered a suit of clothes from his firm, Messrs Lesley and Roberts of 16 George Street, Hanover Square. I was to have a fitting when I could come to London. The suit was to cost £8.8.0 as a trial and the subsequent charge would be £10.10.0.

I thought this fairly steep but the suit worked out very nicely. The cutter, Mr Robinson, was excellent. I thought so then and I've thought so ever since. In 1970, he cut a suit for me as Tom Garrison in *I Never Sang For My Father*, which I played at the Duke of York's. Old Tom was eighty years old in the play and Robbie was persuaded by me to cut the suit loose. It nearly broke his heart. He hadn't changed a bit since 1920 but the price of the suit had.

As the Michaelmas term of 1920 progressed, I continued to live Oxford life to the full. It was a life crowded with meetings of clubs, societies and groups, of luncheons and dinners, and through it all endless talk. I had ears as well as a tongue. But I could not escape the spectre of the 'Schools' that lay ahead, now only a few months away. My work was far behind schedule. The vacations had not produced the required solid reading that I had planned. Not that I wasn't up to the job. My misgivings that I was not up to Balliol standards were just self-pitying hypocrisy. I had done well at school in Canada. I had a fair mind and anyway the examinations were held by the university and not the college. The truth was I lacked the self-discipline that the Oxford system demands. At school, work had been constantly scrutinized, tested and disciplined. I thrived on that method. But without the whip crack, I lay back on the traces. It's a sad admission.

About mid-November, I submitted to Kenneth Bell a 'collection', which was an informal examination on the basis of a Schools paper. By informal, I mean that it was written in my own room without the stress and strain of regular examinations. These were held in an awesome hall called the Examination Schools and candidates were required to wear a dark suit and a white dress-tie. The Schools also included an oral examination, or *viva voce* questioning. It took the courage of F. E. Smith, later the Earl of Birkenhead, to put the *viva* in its proper place. When gently admonished for his obvious lack of preparation on a certain subject, F.E. answered, 'I am here to be examined, not to receive unsolicited advice.' Alas, there are few F. E. Smiths, and I was not one of them.

My 'collection' was handed back to me by Kenneth, with the following notation in red ink: 'One good and interesting answer on the Elizabethan drama; an unfinished answer on Elizabethan archbishops, and that is all! It is most important that you revise a term's work and force yourself by an act of will to write in an examination. I'm sure in your case it is the will which defeats you.'

I spent an evening of contrition, resolution and Scotch with Kenneth, ending in our singing a few 'Gordooleys', my tossing flowerpots into Trinity, and Kenneth donning his gown and gating me for a week. His parting admonition had been: 'It's our purpose here to make you think rather than know, but please remember that in order to think, it is necessary to know!'

My pursuit of knowledge in the long vac had been somewhat impeded by the pursuit of a young lady in Cornwall, to say nothing of the fishing, and this quest seemed at the time to have ended in failure. Now a letter from my father brought bad news of my stepmother, whose health had been poor for some time. I made arrangements to leave for California at the end of the term. In 1920, the trip involved eleven days by ship and trains. My plans for concentrated reading during the vac went out the porthole of a second-class cabin of the *RMS Aquitania*.

I found my stepmother very ill and my father desperately worried. Her condition was breast cancer, which in those days was terminal. After five days, I felt callous leaving them, and I never saw my stepmother again.

In the Hilary term of '21, much of that Oxford life I had been so strongly urged to follow by my brother was dropped. I 'sported my oak' most evenings; that is, bolted the heavy oak door of my room and did my damnedest to catch up with the reading I had neglected. There were two or three London trips that neither helped my work nor my bank account.

Having a chaperon was still the custom for a theatre or dinner dance. That meant the cost of a foursome, no small burden for an undergraduate with a bank book frequently incarnadined. But after some hard work in the Easter vac, admittedly in London, I made progress in my studies.

At the beginning of the Trinity term, five weeks before my Schools in June, I felt fairly confident. Kenneth Bell wasn't quite so sanguine He still thought I should have a dry run at Schools and wait another term for a real try. I assured him I no longer had the jitters. It was my unfortunate sense of immediacy, I suppose. Everything looked fair for a degree in June, a low degree perhaps but an Oxford degree. True, I was rowing in the college eight again, but that was a wise precaution against Oxford torpor, and anyway, my tutor was coaching us.

There came a day about a month before the Schools when I found myself walking up and down the quad with A. L. Smith, the Master. He was patient and kind. There were questions about my work, how it was progressing and what I felt to be my chances in the Schools.

After about half an hour of traversing the quad under the scrutiny of the whole college, the little man paused and said quietly, 'Perhaps it would be best for you and best for the college if you were to go down without facing the examiners.'

'Master,' I asked, 'am I being sent down?'

'No . . . no . . . that decision I leave to you.'

Then and there, I made the decision.

'What about rowing in the eight, Master?'

The man who had rowed at bow in the Head of the River Eight in 1872 answered, 'You may continue to row in the eight.'

As I look back to my Oxford days, my regret that I decided to leave Balliol increases. I had a good but lazy mind. I had frittered away my two years, mistaking information for knowledge and failing to exercise the self-discipline without which Oxford is a waste of time. The Master was a wise old man, and knew that only I could make the decision.

John Betjeman

For me, there were two Oxfords. There was the Oxford of 1916, when I was a boarder at the Oxford Preparatory School (as the Dragon School was still called by old folk) and there was the Oxford of 1925–28 when I was up at Magdalen College.

There was hardly anyone about in my first Oxford. Everyone was away at the Front. We were sent to visit the wounded soldiers who were occupying Somerville and the other women's colleges in bright blue flannel, and we knitted gloves out of string for the sailors on the minesweepers. At that time, the school seemed almost in the country—north of Linton Road there were manifold allotments; east of us, across the narrow Cherwell, were misty meadows and distant elms. To the south, hawthorn hedges made fields between us and Lady Margaret Hall. The way into the shops was westwards. The city was further than we went on foot. The nearest shops were in North Parade—'N.P.', we called it—Gee's, and Twinings the grocers, and Ora Brown, the cheerful lady who sold us sweets.

There was very little traffic then. The infrequent wartime buses down the Banbury Road were worked by gas, housed in a balloon over the top deck. We went everywhere, when we were free, on bicycles, and I spent many a summer evening bicycling round 'the square', as Bardwell Road, Charlbury Road, Linton Road and Northmoor Road were then called.

Most of us could bicycle with our hands in our pockets, slowly zigzagging past the railed-in gardens where tamarisk and forsythia grew; or we would lean against the cream-coloured lamp-posts with their terra-cotta coloured gas-lamps which were placed at infrequent intervals down all the leafy North Oxford roads.

The school was in the redbrick Anglo-Jackson part of North Oxford, which only burst into full beauty when the hawthorn and pink may was in flower. The inner North Oxford—Crick Road, Norham Gardens, Norham Road and the magic, winding Canterbury Road, the cottages and stables by North Parade, and those ecclesiastical-looking houses gathered round the motherly spire of St Philip and St James ('Phil-Jim')—was more haunting, and more daunting. Bicycling down those 'Phil-Jim' roads whose fenced-in gardens had speckled laurels and 'Beware of the Dog' and 'No Hawkers' on their gates, one could glimpse the front-room windows where the widows of Heads of Houses and famous professors sat writing letters in crowded, gaslit rooms. Flowered papers were on the walls and served as backgrounds to photographs in Oxford frames. Hansom cabs still trotted down these roads, taking the aged inhabitants to the dentist in Beaumont Street, or to one of the two railway stations, or shopping at Elliston and Cavell.

In all the wide-roaded silence, the deepest quiet was on Sunday afternoons, when I would bicycle to No. 4 Chalfont Road. There my father's Aunt Lizzie and her husband, John R. Wilkins, ever generous with tea and rock cakes and jam puffs, lived a life entirely unconnected with the university or the school, but closely bound up with the town. My great-uncle was architect to one of the breweries, and did some nice little public houses in a free, Tudor style. He also restored the Clarendon building, and supervised the construction of Professor Dicey's house on the corner of Bardwell and Banbury Roads on behalf of Colonel Edis.

The OPS, or Lynam's as we called the school, prided itself on its freedom. The boys did not have to wear Eton suits on

Sundays and walk in a crocodile, as did the benighted pupils of Summerfields, further up Banbury Road. We could bicycle into the city and look at colleges. Together with my friend Ronnie Wright, the son of a barrister of Tractarian opinions and of a mother who had recently been converted to Rome, we bicycled off to Oxford churches, noticing their liturgical differences. My favourite was St Peter-le-Bailey, which was always empty and always open. I preferred it to the arid Norman revival of St Andrew's Church, which was also very evangelical. We usually ended our explorations at St Aloysius, the Roman Catholic church, where in a side chapel there was a relic of the True Cross, surrounded by candles, polished brass and jewels, which seemed to me very sacred and alarming, as, indeed, did the whole church, with its apse of coloured saints and its smell of incense and many *dévoués* crossing themselves and looking back at us while on their knees. One of our schoolmasters, Gerald Haynes, who had a passion for church architecture—if it was medieval—took us bicycling round the village churches near Oxford, and listened to our accounts of colleges we had explored and chapels we had visited in the university. He liked to take photographs of Norman features in churches, and it was from him that I learned to think that Norman was the only style that mattered, and that Iffley Church was far the most interesting building in Oxford or its vicinity.

Five years later, Oxford—outwardly very little changed, except for an increase in the number of motor cars, so that one had to look to right and left before crossing the Banbury Road or Magdalen Bridge—was a city of pleasure. Schoolfriends from Marlborough had gone to Oxford ahead of me, among them John Edward Bowle, the historian, who had won a Brackenbury Scholarship to Balliol. I was much affected by his outlook on Oxford. He regarded it as an infinitely superior place to Marlborough—and so did I. Dons were to him—as to me—

cleverer and more learned than schoolmasters. He thought
Balliol the cleverest college, and the Balliol dons therefore the
cleverest in the world—I did, too.

I was at Magdalen, and had beautiful panelled eighteenth-
century rooms on the second floor of New Buildings. From
my bed I would hear the Magdalen bells 'sprinkle the quarters
on the morning town'. They led the chorus of quarters chiming
from Merton and New College. I would wait until the fourth
quarter had struck and the bell announced the hour, before
getting up. This was usually ten o'clock, and so I was too late
for breakfast. That did not matter at all.

My tutor was the Reverend J. M. Thompson, a shy, kind,
amusing man, and a distinguished authority on French history.
Rumour had it that he had been defrocked for preaching in
Magdalen Chapel that the miracles were performed by
electricity. I later found out that he was an early modernist in
theology.

By now I was more interested in the type of churchmanship
in a church than in its architecture. I had no Ronnie Wright
to accompany me on my expeditions; instead, one of my closest
friends was Lord Clonmore (now Wicklow), who was an
ordinand at St Stephen's House, Norham Road. We were both
Anglo-Catholics. Through the offices of the Reverend Frederic
Hood (who was then on the staff of Pusey House under the
celebrated Dr Darwell Stone), I was instructed by the Reverend
Miles Sargent in the Catholic faith, which was nothing like the
abbreviated Matins I had enjoyed daily in the school chapel
at Marlborough.

When I left the gentle charge of the Reverend J. M. Thompson, my tutor was C. S. Lewis, who was then in what he would
have called his 'unregenerate days'. Breezy, tweedy, beer-
drinking and jolly, he was very popular with extrovert undergraduates. He found the liturgy very funny, and delighted in
pointing out *non sequiturs* in it; moreover, he ruined Coleridge's
'Kubla Khan' for me by wondering whether the pants in the
line 'As if this earth in fast thick pants were breathing' were

woollen or fur. Now I knew dons were cleverer than any schoolmaster, even than a headmaster, I realized that when Lewis asked me to read three books of 'Paradise Lost', he had not only read them all himself, but had enjoyed them and even knew what they meant.

Oxford was divided for me into two groups; hearties and aesthetes. Hearties were good college men who rowed in the college boat, ate in the college hall, and drank beer and shouted. Their regulation uniform was college tie, college pullover, tweed coat and grey flannel trousers. Aesthetes, on the other hand, wore whole suits, silk ties of a single colour, and sometimes—but only for about a week or two while they were fashionable—trousers of cream or strawberry-pink flannel. They let their hair grow long, and never found out, as I never found out, where the college playing fields were or which was the college barge. Aesthetes never dined in hall, but went instead to the George restaurant on the corner of Corn-market and George Street, where there was a band consisting of three ladies, and where punkahs, suspended from the ceiling, swayed to and fro, dispelling the smoke of Egyptian and Balkan cigarettes. Mr Ehrsam, the perfect Swiss hotelier, and his wife kept order, and knew how much credit to allow us. I was an aesthete.

The chief Oxford aesthete when I went up in 1925 was Harold Acton who, with his brother William, was at Christ Church, but was never seen inside the college in my day. He was a frequenter of restaurants, and his own lodgings were somewhere in the High. Michael Dugdale, another aesthete and a friend of mine at Balliol, always used to walk into Brasenose—an entirely athletic college—with the aid of a stick and limping, because he knew that the athletes would be too sporting to attack a lame aesthete.

Aesthetes used to gather at the very fashionable sherry parties—largely attended by Anglo-Catholic and a certain number of Roman Catholic undergraduates—given on Sundays at noon by George Alfred Kolkhorst, lecturer in Spanish at

Exeter College and later Reader in the university. He had
been born in Chile, which would explain why he knew Spanish,
as I cannot imagine him ever taking the trouble to learn it.
We nicknamed him 'Colonel' Kolkhorst, as he was so little
like a colonel. He was very tall with a slight stoop, and had
rooms on the first floor at No. 38 Beaumont Street. When he
first came up as an undergraduate, the Colonel had been
known as G'ug—the apostrophe, he thought, implied deference,
and gave the impression of a slight yawn when pronounced.
He wore a lump of sugar hung from his neck on a piece of
cotton 'to sweeten his conversation', and at some of his parties
would be dressed in a suit made entirely of white flannel,
waistcoat and all. Though people never got drunk at the
Colonel's parties, it was a habit to form a circle round him and
slowly gyrate, calling out 'The Colonel's tight, the room's going
round!' And we used to stick stamps on his ceiling by licking
them and throwing them up on up-turned pennies. After one
of his merrier sherry parties, the Colonel accompanied Robert
Byron and Lord Clonmore and some other undergraduates to
the top of St Mary Magdalen's Tower in the Cornmarket,
where they sang hymns and began spitting on the people on
the pavement. The Proctors were called and waited at the
bottom of the Tower for the delinquents to descend, which
they eventually did, headed by the Colonel in his white suit.
As a graduate of the university and lecturer in Spanish, he
was immune from punishment, but the others were fined.

The Colonel disliked dons, believing that they took themselves too seriously. He regarded Spanish as hardly a subject
at all, and not worth learning. He thought Cervantes the only
outstanding Spanish author, though he liked the Nicaraguan
poet Ruben da Rio, whose name we would pronounce at sherry
parties with a tremendous rolling of 'r's. The one thing the
Colonel detested above all else was research. It might be
justified in reputable subjects like 'Literae Humaniores' and
biology and the physical sciences, he said, but in Modern
Spanish, a subject with very little literary history, research

meant nothing but scratching around inventing subjects to increase the self-esteem of examining professors, and did no one any good.

If anyone talked about their subject or held forth with a lot of facts at his parties, the Colonel would open his mouth to simulate a yawn, tapping his upper lip as he did so. He carried a little ear trumpet for 'catching clever remarks', but would swiftly put it away and yawn if they were not clever. I never heard of anyone seeing him in Exeter College, and it was a frequent practice of his friends to ask at the Lodge whether the Colonel had been in lately.

Magdalen College, to which I was admitted through the kindness of the President, Sir Herbert Warren, had been the best college—in the social sense—because Edward VIII had been an undergraduate there when Prince of Wales. It had a very famous steward of the Junior Common Room, named Gynes, who saw to it that the undergraduates had the best food and wine when they entertained in their rooms. I remember giving a luncheon party at which constant glasses of Tokay were the only drink from the hors d'oeuvre to the coffee. I must have seemed an impossible person to poor C. S. Lewis, but he had his revenge, for he wrote me a reference when I was trying to become a private schoolteacher which was so double-edged that I withdrew it after my first unsuccessful application for a post.

However, the best college in my time—it probably still is— was Christ Church, known as 'the House'. There, blue blood prevailed; it was the Mecca of all the socially ambitious. Indeed, one undergraduate who had rooms in the college backing on to a public highway, would let down a rope ladder from his windows after the bell in Tom Tower had finished striking its one hundred and one notes—which meant that all college gates were closed. This undergraduate allowed people from other colleges to use his rope ladder if they were acceptable to him. Thus it was said that he had climbed into society by a rope ladder.

There was always an atmosphere of leisure surrounding Christ Church undergraduates. They gave the impression that they were just dropping in at Oxford on their way to a seat in the House of Lords, shortly to be vacated on the decease of their fathers, or that they were coming in for a term or two, but mostly staying away from college in country houses. They hunted, fished and shot. They may even have rode. But I never heard of them playing football or hockey, or even cricket, though cricket was sometimes played in the grounds of country houses within motoring distance of Oxford, and men from 'the House' might have been called upon to swell a village team. Then it was not unusual for a rich undergraduate, and there were many such at the House, to chuck out the Bursar's furniture and all the humdrum college fittings in his rooms, and have the whole place redecorated at his mother's advice and expense. Edward James, for instance, had rooms in Canterbury Quad whose ceilings were black and whose walls were gold, and around the frieze in Trajan lettering ran the words 'Ars longa, vita brevis'. They outstayed Edward's tenure of the rooms.

Of course, there were also ordinary lay undergraduates— that is, those who were neither peers nor very rich—at Christ Church. There was the clever, bespectacled historian from Cornwall, A. L. Rowse, whom I was not to know till later. My chief friend among the laymen was a tow-haired boy from Greshams called Wystan Auden, who was reading English and was tutored by Nevill Coghill of Exeter College. Coghill was an inspiring tutor who rendered Chaucer into readable English, and was a keen producer of Shakespeare at the OUDS.

There must have been dons at Christ Church, too, though apart from Professor Lindemann (later Lord Cherwell, the scientist, and friend of Winston Churchill), and Gilbert Ryle the philosopher, and J. C. Masterman, the senior censor and historian, I do not remember them . . . except for Roy Harrod, a young don who looked about my own age. He, as junior censor, was in charge of undergraduates' behaviour.

Balliol was, as I have mentioned, the cleverest college, but it was more ascetic than aesthetic. Balliol was associated with brains. Our hero Aldous Huxley had been there in rooms papered plain grey, looking out on frosty stars above the Waterhouse block's Scottish baronial turrets. The whole tone of the college was Scottish and frugal, but like all things Scottish, it had a side of unbridled exuberance, reserved for parties. Lampoons would be sung outside the rooms of dons. Fortunately the dons at Balliol were far friendlier to under-graduates than at most other colleges. The don who dominated Balliol was 'Sligger' Urquhart, who held court in summer on a lawn of the garden quad near the dining-hall. He liked people to be well-born, and if possible, Roman Catholic, and he gave reading parties in Switzerland. I only knew him well enough to touch my hat to him, or to give him an oily smile.

Balliol had good scouts, the undergraduates gave good luncheons and teas in their rooms, and it was the college where I had the most friends. Balliol people whom I knew were, like me, not college men, and therefore were to be found in restaurants and other people's rooms. As well as John Edward Bowle, there was Wyndham Ketton-Cremer, Norfolk squire, Old Harrovian, and a gentle pastoral poet much admired by Bowle. An old distich (by Dennis Kincaid, a Balliol wit who was the life and soul of the Colonel's parties) hath it:

> '*John Edward Bowle*
> *Had a superflux of soul.*
> *He was more beautiful than Rima,*
> *But not as beautiful as Ketton-Cremer.*'

Exeter College was for me the headquarters of Anglo-Catholicism, and I had many friends there, too. The dons were mostly approachable and encouraging, like Professor R. M. Dawkins, who had rooms on the ground floor, and appeared delighted to welcome anyone who called on him, whatever his real feelings about the intruders. He preferred, however,

tough sporting men to aesthetes. He was an unconventional
man with a red walrus moustache, freckled bald head and gold
wire spectacles. He was exactly one's idea of the absent-minded
professor, yet nothing escaped him. He was generally called
'Dorks', and was reputed to have known Baron Corvo, though
he never mentioned him to us undergraduates. The fact that
he was Sotheby and Bywater Professor of Byzantine and
Modern Greek was a matter of childlike wonder and delight
to him. Although he was the son of a land-owning family
with military traditions, he was the least military of men. He
had been put into the electrical engineering business in
Chelmsford, but had carried on with modern Greek, regardless.
How he moved from electricity to a Fellowship at Emmanuel
College, Cambridge, is a puzzle. He always thought of himself
as a Cambridge man even after Oxford had made him a
Professor. He once told me you could never depend on the
aesthetic opinions of classical scholars or philosophers—
scientists were far more reliable and humble-minded.

That was my second Oxford. It has lasted long. Still the
colleges retain their individuality. I could have gone on
through every college in Oxford and the halls and theological
colleges, but time and the patience of readers press. I must
conclude with a mention of what has always been my favourite
college—Pembroke, where Dr Johnson's teapot was preserved
in the library. In my day it was still a college you could enter
if the dons liked you. Examinations were not all that important.
Mr Drake, who was the senior tutor, was the greatest authority
on port in England, and Pembroke had the best cellar. The
last Lord Pembroke was at the college in my day and wrote
excellent racing news for the *Cherwell* when I was an editor. I
don't think he bothered much about exams. The Master was
the great Dr Holmes Duddon, the most successful of all Vice-
Chancellors. He had been a popular London preacher at the
fashionable and beautiful Holy Trinity Church, Sloane Street.
He and Mr Drake and Mr Salt, a High Churchman and
Bursar, and dear old Doctor Ramsden, a scientist who kept

silkworms on the mulberries in the Fellows' Garden, made the Pembroke Senior Common Room the most enviable of all. Clipped ivy still grew on the walls and in summer the window boxes were filled with pink geraniums, the college colour. Pembroke retained, of course, its barge when all the 'withits' were building boat houses of brick. With its creeper-hung walls, intimate quads and rich Chapel decorated by Kempe, Pembroke was the best-maintained and most romantic Oxford survival. Even today its new buildings have involved the restoration of little streets adjoining, and no flashy additions. Hurrah!

J.I.M. Stewart

J. I. M. Stewart was born in 1906 and was educated at the Edinburgh Academy and Oriel College, where he took a first class degree in English language and literature in 1928. He lectured at the University of Leeds, was Professor of English at the University of Adelaide from 1935 to 1945, and Lecturer at Queen's University, Belfast from 1946 to 1948. He returned to Oxford as a Student of Christ Church and university lecturer in 1949 and became a Reader in English Literature in the university in 1969. Under his own name he has published fifteen novels, and under the name of Michael Innes more than thirty detective stories. He married in 1932.

In the year 1900 (which was a quarter of a century before I went up to Oriel) there appeared a volume called *Memories of some Oxford Pets by their Friends*. The Sub-Rector of Lincoln, William Warde Fowler, explains in a preface that these essays have been brought together by Mrs Wallace 'to win something for the sick and wounded in the war which has made the past winter such a sad one for us', and that her aim will be the easier to achieve in that 'Mr Blackwell has most kindly consented to undertake the work of publication without any profit to himself'. Warde Fowler urges upon hesitating browsers in Mr Blackwell's shop the consideration that 'animal life is assuredly worth study'.

Numerous persons eminent in their day contribute to this publication. The Right Hon. Professor and Mrs Max Müller report upon their dachshunds; a Mull terrier called Skian is the recipient of an important letter from Dr Birkbeck Hill, greatest of all Johnson scholars; Tom of Corpus is celebrated in an English elegy by Sir Frederick Pollock and in a Latin elegy by Mr Plumer; a poodle called Puffles is commemorated in both verse and prose, and so effectively that in my own time as a senior member of the university his name had been transferred to a distinguished member of the higher clergy, the Suffragan Bishop of Dorchester.

One might expect *Some Oxford Pets*—a descendant of the

keepsake books of the earlier nineteenth century—to contain a good deal of the sentimental and the facetious; in fact it exhibits humour, wit, vivacity, and an unforced lightness of air, and may be regarded as a small document of authentic significance in the history of Oxford taste at the close of Victoria's reign. It pleases me that pride of place in it is given to Oriel Bill. The only illustration, a frontispiece, is a handsome photograph of Bill provided by Mr Soame, who was still in my undergraduate time photographing (gratuitously) those of my contemporaries who were achieving precocious fame at the Union or on the river, or even within the Examination Schools of the university.

Bill was a bulldog, the property (or friend) of A. Wootten-Wootten of Headington and Oriel, with whom he lodged for a time at 15 Oriel Street. When Mr Wootten-Wootten attained to the B.A. degree and departed into the world Bill lingered on amid the scenes and faces he had come to love. In his later years, like other retired Oxford worthies in Headington and similar purlieus of the town, he became a little chary of too frequently dropping in on his old college. For long, indeed, he turned up only for the greater festivals: a habit which unfortunately resulted in a growing addiction to the pleasures of the table. But he continued to know every member of the college, and would go with an Oriel man anywhere, while to all others turning a deaf ear. Having earned a just celebrity not only with the learned and investigating classes but with the citizenry at large, he was at all times able to hail a hansom cab when he required to be driven home. He earned high distinction on the stage when undertaking the part of Launce's dog in an OUDS production of *The Two Gentlemen of Verona*.

The memoir of Oriel Bill—written in Charles Lamb's *Elia* manner and not much below Lamb at his best—was contributed to Mrs Wallace's volume by the Rev. L. R. Phelps, later Provost of the college, one of the first acquaintances I made when, a misdoubting Scottish youth, I entered within its curtilage. Dr Phelps was a hospitable man, who faithfully discharged his duty of entertaining the junior members of his society in bunches and on a systematic basis. Being a good conversationalist in a somewhat allusive mode, however, he took particular pleasure in tête-à-tête occasions with juvenile interlocutors possessed of sufficient miscellaneous reading to know what he was talking about. I must have filled this bill quite well, since I can't recall ever having been in his presence in the company of another undergraduate. And since I was very shy, the Provost may moreover have judged me (fallaciously in fact) incapable of convivial association with my contemporaries, and have been the more inclined benevolently to take me up as a consequence.

Dr Phelps was a venerably bearded man, very liable to inspire even more than an appropriate awe, and when I went to tea with him in the Lodging it was frequently to find him entertaining some scholar more venerable still. At one early tea-party it was the great Dr Paget Toynbee, then regarded in Oxford as the first of living authorities on Dante; and Dr Toynbee received a tremendous dressing-down for having turned up on a brief visit to the university without having included dress clothes in his stock of attire. The tea ceremony was itself intimidating, rather in the fashion that a later generation associated with the receiving of that civil refection from the hands of Miss Ivy Compton-Burnett. The equipage included china which had perhaps belonged to the Provost's grandmother. Certainly he cherished it very much. He began by letting fall into each saucer, with a maximum of precision, a single drop of hot water from a heavy silver jug held in an aged but well-poised hand. I supposed this hydrostatic performance to be in aid of fractionally increasing friction or adhesion between saucer and cup, thereby minimizing the risk of humiliating misadventure on the part of a guest doing a balancing act on his knees.

But the Provost, although adept at giving an appearance of leisure to social occasions, was not by nature of a sedentary habit, and he had developed numerous resources for speeding the departure of those young men (always a majority, whatever their background) who were unable to get to their feet and take their leave. Thus at tea-time he would lead the conversation towards some athletic topic, from this to the college games field, and from this again to the subject of badgers—which he would aver, quite baselessly, to have established a set endangering the cricket pitch. He would then recall Sir Thomas Browne's holding in debate whether or not badgers have longer legs on one side than the other, this the more readily to scamper round hills. Next, he would suddenly recall that a portrait of a badger hung somewhere in the Lodging, from which the truth of this matter might conceivably be verified. The picture would be located after a walk through the ramifying house; the badger would be seen to be equipped as other quadrupeds are; and then one would discover that the picture hung beside the Provost's front door, which stood open before one. The proper words would be spoken, and one was out in the triangular public space which the college was later going to persuade the municipality to give a name to as Oriel Square.

Dr Phelps's after-dinner technique was simpler. He would wait until, from the adjacent Tom Tower, Christ Church began to bang out the hundred-and-one peals with which—with some justification immemorially antique—it assaults the city nightly at five minutes past nine o'clock. The Provost would thereupon stand up and shamelessly declare: 'Ah, my dear boys! The witching hour of twelve has struck.'

I have said that the Provost was no sedentary man. He was in fact a formidable pedestrian, and he marched me over as much of the countryside round Oxford as I have ever traversed since. On Sundays, however, his favourite walk was merely up the hill to Headington, where at that time there was situated what I imagine was still called the Workhouse. He had sat on the Poor Law Commission of 1905–1909, and in vagrancy in particular he maintained a keen interest. So we would set off of an afternoon for a chat with the tramps. The walk through Oxford could be slightly embarrassing, since the Provost was given to greeting totally strange passers-by as a squire might greet his cottagers. To men he would raise his blackthorn stick and call out 'Good day to you, my master!' and to women he would touch the brim of his large speckled straw hat. On these Sunday expeditions I felt I ought to wear a hat myself, and as there was no time to doff it to every female thus encountered I was reduced to the brim-touching technique too, and self-consciously felt it to be extremely ludicrous. The tramps, however, were enormous fun, since Dr Phelps possessed the art of drawing them into a free if not very articulate conversation. There was one, from Yorkshire, who claimed to remember the Brontës—and who, it was evident, did authentically remember legends about them.

Dr Phelps was himself good at remembering, and on the walk back to college might entertain me with what I was required to receive as first-hand reminiscences of Matthew Arnold and John Henry Newman. There was frequently a satirical slant to these, particularly when he was dealing with Arnold. One story, much detail of which I forget, was of Arnold's driving out to Blenheim to call on the Duke of Marlborough, entangling his boot inextricably with some patent unfolding step of the conveyance, and writhing helplessly before a line of frozen flunkeys, with the duke himself looking on, equally immobile, at the top of an enormous flight of steps. It was not, I think, the Provost himself who told me how, as a very junior fellow of the college, he was despatched with a group of more senior Anglican clergy having the delicate task of congratulating a former fellow on becoming a prince of the Holy Roman Catholic and Apostolic Church. Young Phelps broke the ice by advancing upon the new Cardinal of St George in Velabro with outstretched hand and the words, 'Well done, Newman, well done!' I believe anecdotes like this a little startled me, Arnold and Newman standing in my mind as the chief glories, by no means thus to be frivolously dealt with, of the not particularly distinguished college in which I found myself.

Phelps and his successor in the Provostship, my moral tutor

W. D. Ross, a much more intellectual man, are the only dons
I can remember taking much account of. Ross told me at
some brief beginning-of-term interview, when I had no doubt
been talking pretentiously about my reading and opinions,
that it seemed to him that a great deal of nonsense was written
about literature. Because he said this at once diffidently and
with authority (a not impossible combination) I received it as
a maxim at once, and have applied it with great benefit in
my dealings with critical expatiation ever since.

The undergraduates of the 1920s belonged as definitely to a
pre-revolutionary era as they did to a post-war one. It had
been widely believed that such a cataclysm as the Kaiser's War
would be bound to bring radical changes to Oxford. In some
colleges the dons held a nervous fear that a returned young
soldiery, of whom there were bound to be many, must prove
unruly and licentious. They even recruited, under various
academic disguises, officers from the Brigade of Guards as
experts in disciplinary action. But in fact nothing disruptive
occurred. The demobbed warriors proved, if anything, more
orderly and industrious than the boys straight from school.
There was a general disposition simply to get things going
again, to pick up old threads. Within a few years everything
was re-established and as it had been. The Oriel I entered a
few days after my nineteenth birthday in 1925 can have
differed in no marked particular from the Oriel of twenty
years before. The social composition of the place was the same:
preponderantly public school, and taking the manners and
assumptions of gentlemen's sons for granted. It was also taken
for granted that, although there were menservants around to
empty our slops and carry meals and coal-scuttles up to our
rooms, we were essentially schoolboys still, and to be governed
accordingly. We were segregated from the other sex both by
sundry regulations and on a curiously matter-of-course basis
which was a hang-over from the way we had been put through

school. 'Womanizing' of a low sort classed a man as unspeak-
able; romantic attachments and even cautious physical experi-
ments—but all preferably disastrous—with girls in distant
places and during vacations were admitted and occasioned
mild awe; but one risked ridicule by a bare mention of the
women's colleges already flourishing in the university. We
were locked up at night. We had to attain a fixed quota of
attendances in the college chapel under penalty of being
punished in various annoying and trivial ways. There was a
further odd segregation when we dined in hall, the clever men
having to sit at one table and the other men at others. In the
main, I suppose, this last ordinance led to people the more
readily finding themselves in congenial society. But it enhanced
the notion of scholars and commoners being races apart, and
its application in individual cases could be absurd. I can
recall Ronald Syme, a mature student from New Zealand who
was later to become Camden Professor of Ancient History,
having thus to associate nightly in a sort of dunces' gallery
exclusively with callow youths whose conversational range
was confined to matters of athletic or social concern. In this
instance, indeed, the result was pleasingly comical, the future
Sir Ronald being unable to conceive of any human being as
other than passionately interested in classical antiquity—and
talking uninterruptedly, with brilliance and charm, in the
confidence of this fond persuasion.

My own acquaintance were a mixed lot in point alike of
ability and temperament, but rather fell down in terms of any
broad social spectrum. Oriel didn't much go in for the sons of
very wealthy people, and it did harbour the sons of a good
many very poor ones. This latter fact, admirable in its way, I
suspect to have been of the Provost's contriving. One of his
unlikelier stories was of the college's Governing Body once
having contemplated pursuing Thomas Hardy for libel on the
ground that a vignette on the title-page of *Jude the Obscure*
seemed to represent our front quad, and might thus suggest
that it had been by one of his own praepostorial predecessors

that Jude Fawley had been insolently repulsed. Dr Phelps was himself a Carthusian, and Carthusians were prominent among the public school boys who formed the bulk of the college's undergraduate population. But his interest in what used to be called the 'social question' (and rather more a deep charity hidden away in him) made him vigilant to have some genuinely poor scholars around. I remember one contemporary of mine who, having written to him artlessly and from an obscure situation to inquire whether residence at Oxford could be managed on (I think) £30 a year, found himself railroaded into the college at once. He attained in later life to a distinguished position in the profession of letters.

Oxford, like every ancient university, began as an informal association of poor scholars, and for centuries there was almost nobody else around. Later, when the colleges turned substantially into preserves of the prosperous, the penniless lingered on as sizars and the like, and finally as boys living on small scholarships and exhibitions and charitable grants. This didn't in my own time make any sort of edifying spectacle. Considerable gifts of the spirit and intellect are required to counter severe economic disadvantage within a community, and in Oriel as in every other college there were a few young men whose poverty cut them off from too much that was going on. A marked amelioration in this state of affairs has been one of the major gains of the mid-twentieth century. Plenty of people are hard up. But below a certain minimum of subsistence nobody is depressed. If you are poor you at least have plenty of company.

In 1925 it didn't much help those without money that money went a long way. The majority of us, living on modest allowances from fathers in the professions and services and so on, pursued a course of life which would now be regarded as within the reach only of the opulent. We treated each other to quite elaborate luncheon parties in our rooms; dined at the George (where there was the excitement of watching the current celebrities, headed by Harold Acton, come and go with considerable exhibitionistic flair) or drove out to the Spread Eagle at Thame, where Mr John Fothergill afforded us a grand sense of *grande cuisine*, with bills to match. We spent quite a lot of time (it seems incredible today) in expensive clothes, and our shoes came from a superior shop in the Turl. We smoked cigarettes rolled in black paper, or tipped with gold, or in some similar way distinguished from the Gold Flake of the common herd. The pictures on our walls had been done one at a time by artists favourably noticed in sixpenny weeklies. For most of us, of course, there was an honest shoe-string element in the hinterland of all this magnificence. I myself used to get by on the strength of purchasing Francis Meynell's latest Nonsuch Press books in Edinburgh at the end of a vacation and selling them eight weeks later for a larger sum to Mr Sanders in Oxford High Street. The profit paid for a railway ticket home, and there I'd sit down and do some of the work I'd neglected amid the pleasures of university life. This just kept my chin above water as what an earlier generation called a reading man. And all this was very normal and unremarkable.

I sometimes wonder why I don't look back on that life with more affection. One reason must reside in the simple fact that the undergraduate's is in many respects a difficult condition: a state of affairs doubtless constant from generation to generation, and connected with the general ignominy of growing up. One can get awfully glum. Norman Cameron, whom I had known on a neighbourly basis at home, and who had rooms across the staircase from mine in Oriel's front quad, had a habit of breaking in on me in the small hours, making enough noise to wake me up. He would then simply stand and gaze at me in unfathomable dejection. I had no difficulty in matching this mood at once, and after some five minutes of such mute communion Norman would shamble away again, closing the door very softly, as if I were still asleep. His depression may have been enhanced because his scholarship was in some way connected with a Bible clerkship, which meant that he had to appear regularly in the college chapel for the purpose of reading the lessons. His perception of the world's sadness at times a little seduced him from wholly temperate courses, and there was an occasion upon which he advanced to the lectern and pronounced the words, 'Here beginneth the Gospel according to St George.' The Provost from his stall helpfully ejaculated, 'John, boy, John!' But Norman, almost as if he were a scholar in the most senior sense, was reluctant to admit error in a matter of fact. 'Here beginneth the Gospel according to St George,' he reiterated firmly. 'In the beginning was the Word . . .' And he read on in the rumbling sleepy voice which I can still hear when I read his verse.

Twenty years after going down from Oriel I returned to Oxford as a college tutor. Once more a war had ended in a recent past; once more there was a general air of picking up the threads again; once more the returned warriors were of serious and industrious mind. This time, however, radical changes were evident—and it was evident, too, that radical changes were going to continue. As with a largely devastated city, the fabric of British society had to be built up again; much of it would not be as before; to such transformations as came, the university would have to respond. As might be expected amid so much entrenched tradition and assumption as obtains in Oxford, some of these responses were not of the briskest. For example, who was now to come to the place? The colleges, being richly endowed self-governing and self-perpetuating corporations, were inclined to regard this as their own affair, and the university (which could still be viewed as little more than the colleges sitting round a table) was slow to increase the say it had in the matter. Eventually it took some action. There was no need to change the formal position, since already a college could take into residence only persons whose educational qualifications the university deemed adequate. By discreetly moving this test a little away from near-zero the university eventually gained a larger control of the situation, and to the effect of very significantly raising the standard of entrance. Other factors no doubt contributed to this. Among the younger dons now around there were many whose minds had been formed within new climates of opinion; and the competitiveness fostered by a collegiate system began to exercise itself in comparatively new fields—the old talent-scouting techniques being modified to achieve effective operation in schools hitherto regarded as totally obscure. As a result of all this—it may be bluntly said—no men's college is any longer noticeably cluttered up with hopelessly thick or even incorrigibly idle youths from privileged homes. Looking back on the 1920s—I hope with not too jaundiced an eye—I am convinced that here has been a large change indeed. And as universities are places of learning and education it is an important change too.

It is quite as important, certainly, as the change in sexual *mores* ('the sexual revolution') which so frequently arrests the attention of newspaper moralists. Here is a tricky field, all the same, and towards the many young people who demand fresh liberties upon it (and they are indeed numerous, although I doubt whether they would get far on the brute basis of majority rule) three fairly distinct schools of thought would appear to have formed. The first is the forthright Christian one, which requires no comment. The second inclines to the view (for it talks like that) that sex is a good thing, since it has a composing effect when achieved, and returns a man refreshed to his books. The third says that sex is a bad thing—or bad in the context being considered—since it is at best distracting and a waste of time, and at worst productive of nervous break-down and even total failure in the Examination Schools.

Both these latter ways of thinking seem to me trivial and absurd, but I admit this with diffidence, having no more sage comment of my own. I very much doubt whether my tutor at Oriel, an immeasurably deep Elizabethan scholar who was seldom clear about my identity, ever gave serious thought to my sexual life. *Ne sutor* (he would have said with the air of inexpressible erudition he could lend to the most banal quotation)—*ne sutor ultra crepidam.* Who goes with who, the bedclothes say—or, rather, the whole spirit of the age determines; and the matter is perhaps one which teachers within their colleges had best leave alone. It is sometimes averred that Oxford tutors today are inclined to go along with their pupils in overvaluing facile sexual activity. I don't know whether this is in fact so. But to assume that if a young man or woman is unhappy or depressed or not working well it must be because of the failure of some sexual nutrient, so that it is one's duty to the young person to suggest, if only by subtle implication, that it is his or her business to go out and do a quick shop around: to act thus must be to risk doing mischief in a gratuitous way. Rather than that I'd myself prefer to take up an uncompromising Victorian point of view.

The cautious stages by which young men of twenty-one or twenty-two were relieved from the indignity of being put under lock and key at night differed, I imagine, from college to college. In Christ Church in 1949 I was still collecting an irregular sort of gate-money as a consequence of the survival of this antique practice. One of my windows gave on a garden easy of access; it was my wholesome habit to leave the upper sash of this window open at night; and through it would jack-knife young men whose small change tumbled from their pockets in the process. Since they seldom paused to pick up the coins, these were still there when I came into college in the morning. It is my hope—but memory grows dim—that I applied them to some charitable purpose. Eventually this source of revenue dried up, no doubt upon the discovery of some more amusing and hazardous way of climbing within bounds. The business of locked gates was partly a matter of normal security such as any prudent householder would observe, but it was also bound up, of course, with the problem of ladies in college. At what hour does a female presence become indecorous; at what stroke of the clock does virtue waver and libidinousness grow bold? Serious men, charged as deans or senior tutors with the harrassing responsibility of preserving both good behaviour and good feeling among several hundred closely stacked-up youths of vigorous enterprise and spirit, have been obliged gravely to perpend these ludicrous problems.

The minor problem of compulsory chapel-going was easier to solve, and again, it is to be supposed, the solution came about piecemeal round the university.

> '*Be wise,*
> *Ye Presidents and Deans, and to your Bells*
> *Give seasonable rest; for 'tis a sound*
> *Hollow as ever vex'd the tranquil air . . .*'

Wordsworth's vigorous injunction, written in 1805, was heeded at last, with what consequences for the devotional life of the university it would be hard to determine. Nobody could any longer be constrained to listen to a Norman Cameron or a Provost Phelps, speaking with those angelic tongues lent to them by the Prayer Book and the Authorized Version of the Bible. People now sought out these things only if they spontaneously wanted them. In Oxford, the clergy apart, it had become difficult to be religious without enthusiasm.

The quality of undergraduate life 'then and now' is a topic that can be very variously pronounced upon by elderly persons in reminiscent mood. Mr Christopher Hollis, who went up to Balliol in 1920, has lately expressed the opinion that his contemporaries at Oxford lived fuller and more enjoyable lives than their successors can be observed to do today. I incline to the opposite view, while feeling at the same time that we may both err in positing any significant change between one generation and the next. I seem to recall another contemporary, Mr Anthony Powell's Nicholas Jenkins, reflecting that the undergraduate condition is characteristically somewhat melancholy at any time. This may well be the truth. The undergraduate's, after all, is the period of Yeats's

'*distress*
Of boyhood changing into man.'

Angus Wilson

Angus Wilson was born in 1913 and spent part of his childhood in South Africa, his mother's home. He was educated at Westminster School and Merton, where he took a second class degree in Modern History in 1935. The following year he became a librarian in the Reading Room at the British Museum, and after working at the Foreign Office during the war he was deputy to the Superintendent of the Reading Room from 1949 to 1955. He began to write in 1946 because, he says, he had 'decided he needed an extra interest in life'. His many novels have been translated into sixteen languages, and one of them, Late Call, *was successfully serialized on television. He has been Professor of English Literature at the University of East Anglia since 1966. He reviews and lectures widely.*

None of my family had been to Oxford. Nor to Cambridge, for that matter. Save in the expression 'Cambridge blue', I do not remember to have heard that university mentioned until I was sixteen or seventeen. No other university, of course, was ever spoken of. We were essentially the sort of middle-class family that reposed upon 'good' English public schools. My grandfather had come to one all the way from Scotland in the 1850s, and my father in the 1870s. All my brothers, save my delicate third brother, had been at such schools between 1900 and 1917. The first thing my family asked about any man was what school he had been at. With a decent public school behind you and what they called 'a little social pull', a man could get an equally decent post in the City or in the colonies, and of course service officers had no need of universities. If a boy was especially brainy, or there was a tradition in the family of going into the Church ... Otherwise a good public school was all you needed.

The whole of this middle class has, I suppose, now entirely disappeared. Already, by the time my brothers came back from the Great War in 1918, a public school education by itself, without a little capital, was ceasing to be such a miraculous passport. Public schoolboys, including two of my brothers, acted as supers on the sets at Elstree or sold Electrolux vacuum-cleaners from door to door. After 1930, one of the tragedies of the Depression, as seen from Kensington and Eastbourne (my family viewpoints), was that public schoolboys were coming to be 'almost a drug on the market'. Luckily for me (in this respect only, let me hasten to say) my mother had died in spring 1929 when I was fifteen and so, in the Michaelmas term of 1932, when I was just turned nineteen, I went up to Merton College, Oxford.

The connection of events seems fortuitous but was direct. In the first place, had my mother been alive, her small capital (diminished by endless loans to my brothers and gifts to my father) would have been needed for her support. In the second place, her colonial pride in her father's self-made success, usually played down after decades of Kensington and South Coast rentier snobbery, would have probably asserted itself against the idea of my going to Oxford on a private income, even if it could have been afforded. She might have scraped and saved (as only she knew how) to send me there had I secured the closed scholarship from Westminster to Christ Church for which I entered. But I failed to satisfy the examiners. If I try now to recall how, I remember only that I may have made in my viva what I thought witty but what must have been insufferably superior remarks about these very South African maternal ancestors of mine to Patrick Gordon-Walker, later a Labour Cabinet Minister but then a young Christ Church don. And so I only got to Oxford as a commoner at Merton by the aid of my mother's capital which she had left me in her will—reasonably, since she had already helped my elder brothers and I was thirteen years younger than the youngest of them.

Through the enmeshment of family trustees and unpaid family debts to my mother, the sum that I finally received was a good deal smaller than she had reason to think she had left me; but it was enough to give me £300 a year at Oxford on top of my tuition fees, my college payments and my expenses in vacations. It was as my second brother, a headmaster of a preparatory school, who would dearly have loved to have been

ANGUS WILSON 93

at Oxford himself, quite rightly said, a good income. I used, in later days, remembering the chronic impecuniosity of my family, to congratulate myself on having left Oxford with no debts. It was a self-deceiving congratulation, since £300 a year for term-time pleasures alone, in the deflation of the mid-'thirties, allowed me to live in a way almost deserving the popular description 'like a lord'.

Perhaps I should briefly describe this manner of living, since it formed the rather pleasurable material basis of my three years at Oxford. Some part of it was derived from what years of living with my father had taught me was 'a good life'. This principally consisted in eating out at restaurants and having 'good food' as often as possible. I think that I ate in college only in the first two weeks of those three years—and that out of a fear of the consequences of not doing so. This fear was part of the general fear of communal college life that I felt in my first term, for, as I shall describe, coming from a London day school, I half-seriously clothed college life at first with all the terrors of boarding school life that I had derived from stories describing Eton under Keate in the 1820s, or, at best, Rugby under Arnold in the 1850s. In fact, I *was* acting against college regulations by not fulfilling a certain number of dinners in hall; but, as I never 'signed off', I paid in full for dinners every night of my three years and consumed none of them, so the college authorities were the richer by some hundreds of dinners not eaten but paid for. It might have occurred to me that *this* was an example of inherited prodigality, but it never did; I saw it as the only way of avoiding 'the too appalling food and company'. In those first three weeks I had seen people throw bread at each other and had anticipated that before term was out this would have ended in bodily assaults. I had also received a garbled account of 'sconces'. I had not understood that these were forfeits by which you had to pay for other people's beers (something I should like to have done) but I thought rather that they were penalties in which beer was forcibly poured down one's throat. In any case the food, by the

standards my father had given me from the Café Royal and
the Trocadero, was vile, worse than that served at my brother's
prep school, which was the nadir of my father's scale of feeding.
After the first three weeks, I ate out in restaurants.

My closest circle, especially in the early days, was a number
of friends from Westminster—some at Christ Church, some at
New College and elsewhere. It was natural that we should eat
together as often as college regulations allowed. We soon found
that the best food was at the George—it served that sort of
good semi-French cuisine that still existed in the best English
provincial restaurants before the war, before ignorant and
pretentious 'international' menus based on deep freezes had
led to our present sad state of affairs. But whereas I think my
friends ate out only on those evenings when they did not have
to pay for college hall, I ate out every evening, often sitting by
myself, elaborately consuming Sole Mornay and Meringue
Chantilly with a book propped up against the vase of flowers
that ornamented the table. I (and the others) could not by any
means regularly afford the George and we ate at assorted
restaurants, cafés and 'ladies' tearooms'. I remember no other
place that seemed 'good' save a restaurant in the Cornmarket
where for a time they served excellent asparagus omelettes. As
to drink, my father had years ago foresworn alcohol as a result
of near cirrhosis of the liver, and I therefore knew little of
wines. Only one of our circle, coming from a wealthier family,
was used to drinking wine at all regularly. I think this lack of
regular wine drinking was much more common in middle-
class homes of some pretension in the inter-war years not only
than now but than it had been in late Victorian times. At
restaurants we drank normally gin and tonic; and, in our own
rooms, a great deal of dry sherry (a peculiarly disgusting habit,
I think now). On occasions of evening celebrations and parties
we also drank, as I remember, port and liqueurs, especially
cointreau. This curiosity becomes explicable when I reveal
that the cocktail for smart parties—we drank it in large
quantity on my twenty-first birthday—was a White Lady (gin

and cointreau in suitable proportions). Later—from the summer term of my first year—when I had come to know the life better and had no more fears of college, I used to give luncheon parties in my rooms. The food for these was very good. I got to know the college chef, who understandably liked appreciation. His speciality was a first-class crème brulée. With these luncheons I provided wine—by whose advice I can't remember, it became habitually 'Liebfraumilch'.

On top of this rather extravagant expense upon food, I smoked regularly about thirty-five or forty cigarettes a day, very costly small flat Turkish cigarettes called Melachrino, which I carried about with me in tins of a hundred. Occasionally I tried to economise by changing to Abdullah. But these seemed very ordinary, even though I smoked them in a long cigarette holder from which the stubs could be ejected by pressing a little button—so far as I know, a new amusing device. From my second year on, I also purchased from Hall Bros. in the High Street a good number of canary-coloured woollen waistcoats with brass buttons, a lot of foulard spotted scarves, and a pleasing selection of bottle green, maroon and dark crimson velvet ties (ordinary ties, not bow ties). These added a touch of elegance to my regulation undergraduate grey flannels, sports coats and umbrellas, that deceptively might have suggested to a stranger that I belonged to a smart Oxford set. There was, however, no intention of deceit in these sartorial accessories; it was simply that for the first time I could buy the clothes I wanted and I knew that I wanted these. The rest of my money went on books from Blackwell's—a good number both new and second-hand—which I paid for on account at the end of each term. I do not remember to have paid anything towards furnishing, save for a pair of hideous orange and apricot shot silk cushion covers which I had made because my rooms 'lacked colour'.

All this must sound, and is, very small beer; but I state it because I remember my Oxford years always against a sense of pleasing material sufficiency and comfort. It would not have been so, I think, if I had gained that scholarship and gone to Christ Church, for then I should fairly quickly have made friends far richer than I was and rapidly have got into debt. As it was, I only came to know a few such people much later when I joined the OUDS—by which time my pattern of life was set and they were merely a handful among a varied circle of acquaintances. At Merton, I was probably financially better off than most of the undergraduates, and could make my own standards. I count this as one of the most important of the many advantages Merton gave to me.

At first I didn't feel it so, however. All my Westminster friends were at other colleges. There *was* a very small rich set at Merton, and in my first weeks they made a great deal of drunken noise on many nights. As, with my father's assistance, I had chosen some excellent rooms over the Junior Common Room, I noticed this noise particularly. It seemed the blood-curdling prelude to heaven knew what roastings and defenestrations. I was very 'pansy' in manner and I was very conscious of it. The other new people who seemed out of it all were different. They came from various parts of the North and Midlands of England. A few of them were to become my close friends. But in those first weeks, I could as easily have confessed my loneliness and alarms to them as a warthog can communicate his fears of lion to a herd of zebras. Such people as visited me in my rooms came to ask me if I intended to play this or that athletic game—something I had never been expected to do in my last years at Westminster. Of course, I was not really expected to do so at college, but it all added to my feeling that I had joined Stalky and Co.

I remember that for some weeks I did not dare to stay in my rooms in the afternoons for fear I should be identified as an aesthete or a swot. I went for long and tedious walks into the countryside, and, only after one desperate and frozen visit to the pathetic little Oxford zoo, did I settle down to a programme of browsing the early afternoon away at Blackwell's, followed by china tea and walnut layer cake at Fuller's tea-room. Apart from my evenings spent with my Westminster friends, that first term was hell, in particular because I had greatly looked forward to unlimited reading of medieval history and now I found that because I had to take Pass Mods, my days were spent in elementary classes in Latin and Economics that seemed to have transported me back at least two years in time to the school world before School Certificate.

It was not surprising that, with my lifelong capacity for psychosomatic illnesses, I went down with jaundice after Christmas and most ungratefully told my father and my brother that I didn't want to return to Oxford. However, they nobly persuaded me against their financial interest, and I came back to what were to be uniformly happy (though not ecstatic) years.

I must digress here for a paragraph or two to say how mysterious I find that kind of permanent identification with Oxford and Oxford things that so many men appear to make. When I read of the Oxford days of Cyril Connolly or of Evelyn Waugh, I stand in amazement at the hypnotic effect that the university had upon them. It might have been so for me, too, I suppose, if I had been at Balliol. I had already been much influenced by one very Oxford-struck Balliol man, the historian John Edward Bowle, who had taught me history in my last two years at Westminster. He, I think, has never been wholly content away from Oxford, where he now resides. Other friends of mine, often successful and distinguished, seem to look forward to frequent visits to Oxford to regale themselves afresh with high-table gossip—happy those few of them who have All Souls Fellowships or dining rights at their colleges. Such lasting enchantment is clearly not confined to Oxford, for the very type of such men seems to have been E. M. Forster at King's. Nor is it wholly to do with the more celebrated or grander colleges. I count these friends happy in this curious pleasure. Clearly they are more discriminating than those who live for visits to their old schools. But I don't at all understand how their affections became so fixed. I was flattered and

pleased when the Warden of Merton invited me to dine at
High Table a few years ago; I was also delighted to be invited
to speak at Westminster School. I live quite a lot in the past
and to visit at intervals places which bring memories alive gives
me great pleasure; but I greatly dislike an exclusive call upon
my affections or loyalties of any one of these past places—
Sussex, South Africa, Oxford, Kensington, Provence, Bloomsbury, East Anglia and so on—over the others. Yet for many
people Oxford clearly has a magic that never leaves them.

It may be that a great part of these men and women had
hoped or intended to become Oxford dons and make their
lives there. I notice that they have in common with my Oxford
don friends a kind of mythology that underlies their general
gossip, in which the names of Oxford 'figures'—Bowra,
Sparrow, Berlin, David Cecil, Rowse, Trevor-Roper and
many others—play a continuous part, standing all the time for
something mysteriously more than the remarkable men who
possess them. This is, of course, to be expected if you are part
of the Oxford set-up, but if, in fact, your contacts are confined
to a certain number of visits a year, it seems strange. It is not
just gossip, it is the sense such people, who have known
Oxford's magic, convey that 'thought' and 'civilization' and
the 'real world' are inextricably bound up with the university.
I had no idea or hopes of becoming a don. I aimed, at first,
rather vaguely at schoolteaching and then later, more definitely,
at getting a job in the British Museum. In any case, until I
was forty, I suppose, I could not have imagined the centre of
my life outside London. Therefore I never saw Oxford at any
time as other than a place of temporary sojourn. I talked a
great deal and listened to a great deal of talk about politics
and literature and history; but, as I shall show, it had little
to do with what was being thought in serious academic circles
in Oxford. Dons were either the few who had things to tell
me about English history that interested me, or the many more
whose first lectures in the term I attended to be reduced to
painful suppressed giggles by what seemed to me the immensely

comic quirks with which they delivered their boring discourses.
I had to leave a lecture of the Regius Professor because my
laughter set rattling the form on which I was sitting. Anything
interesting I could find in books. The idea of knowing dons
socially never entered my head. There was a famous university
figure at Merton called Garrod who entertained undergraduates. I was clearly not the sort of undergraduate he
entertained, for he never invited me; but I also am clear that it
never occurred to me to get myself invited to his famous teas.
I had met both John Sparrow and Maurice Bowra when I was
a schoolboy, through John Edward Bowle, and had found them
charming and entertaining; but, once again, I do not think
that I even remembered that they were connected with
Oxford when I was there.

Some part of this failure to respond to Oxford's importance
I am pleased about. I was not an ambitious young man, using
the university and its contacts for worldly advancement. When
I meet such young men occasionally—presidents or secretaries
of this or that—I am repelled and saddened, for they seem to
be wasting their youth in exploiting it for their adult years. At
least, my life at Oxford, however small and self-satisfied and
over-glib, was enjoyed every minute for itself. But there was
great loss in it. Not the loss of not having known famous dons,
but something that this implies—a lack of humility before
knowledge, and more still a lack of capacity to listen to difficult
thinking, a protective irony and frivolity that lost me more in
power to reason and evaluate than they saved me from boredom
and pretension and intellectual snobbery. I was right, as were
my friends, to think that we could supply sophistication and
wit and elegance of living as good if not better than these
distinguished dons could provide. But to see this was to see
only the superficial. What I missed was the capacity to think
hard and painfully; to have learned this would have been
worth supporting a great deal of the cult-nonsense that
surrounded Oxford's famous men. Ironically enough, the
failure of my undergraduate life at Oxford which irks me most

is something quite else. It is the fact that the architectural beauty of Oxford largely passed me by. I attended, I remember, a series of fascinating lectures on architectural history delivered by Goodheart Rendel at the Ashmolean, but it never occurred to me to look for what I had seen on the lantern screen in the streets and quads. I was not wholly damned, for I always felt a visual excitement in seeing the Queen's College, and I was quite right. I remember moments of transported joy in combined architectural and natural scenery—walking in the Botanical Gardens, in Addison's Walk, sitting one hot day preparing for Schools beneath the walls of Merton Fellows' Garden. But, in general, Oxford's visual beauty passed me by. Yet in fact this was not so serious, for twenty years later architecture began to exercise an increasing spell over me, and now a stay in Oxford is a continuous visual delight. To think about difficult things and listen to difficult thinking, let alone to express it, I shall never now learn.

I must content myself with the thought that I probably never could have done, and had I tried to do so at Oxford I should simply have crushed such originality and capacity for *aperçus* as I have beneath a dead weight of received thinking. Perhaps so, probably not. One thing offers some explanation. Oxford in the early 'thirties was not in that sense, I think, a 'great' time. Of all the people I associated with in the OUDS only Sir Terence Rattigan and Peter Glenville have been figures of real influence in the theatre; most of the other actors and producers have faded out. Although I debated politics privately endlessly, I was not a Union man, beyond attending some famous debates. Yet I do not think that any of the undergraduates of my time have achieved political fame, unless it be John Freeman, whom I knew quite well, but I don't think he had political ambitions then. There are probably many well-known people who were Oxford undergraduates whom I never knew; but of my friends of those days the best known are most certainly women—Barbara Jackson (then Barbara Ward), Sally Chilver, the Principal of Lady Margaret Hall.

The high 'twenties of Waugh and John Betjeman and Cyril Connolly and Harold Acton were behind us. The 'thirties poets of the Left, too, had gone down by the time I arrived. Only the war itself, in fact, lay ahead. It is against this background that I must briefly sketch the various positive ways in which I gained from Oxford. My London sophistication and my Westminster schooling and my camp carry-on attached me to the OUDS and past Oxford; Merton and the friends I made there from working-class homes in the Midlands and the North attached me to politics and the Left. The latter because it was a new experience was the more important; yet by now I should find it hard to say how much of either is left in me in the form in which I received them then. Very little, I think.

The central thread of my university life began with the small group (three or four) of Westminster friends at other colleges and remained with it to the end. We knew each other's families before we went up. We stayed at each other's houses in the vacation. We continued to know each other into adult years; and the only other survivor of the group, D. P. Walker, the eminent scholar of the Warburg Institute, is still a close friend of mine. Three or four other undergraduates became part of our group, although none of them, in fact, through me. Two of us were historians; two studying French and German literature; two medicine. None, and it was a serious intellectual loss to me, philosophy. Otherwise, this mixture of subjects was good. It led me, for example, to read a good deal of French, and even German, literature which I should not otherwise have done; and started, in French at any rate, a lifelong habit. It gave me some acquaintance with the current problems in biology and medicine. As we none of us studied English literature, this (and in particular the English novel) became our lingua franca. I read a prodigious number of the great English novelists. For all this I am very grateful, although it can hardly have helped my concentration on my history studies. We spent evenings reading plays together over port or madeira. The standard of intelligence among our small group varied greatly as did our centres of study. One friend, in particular, who died in the war, had a strong personality but rather small reasoning powers. Humour, therefore, and above all humorous gossip and amateur psychologizing, inevitably loomed large, for they dissolved any mental disparities. We were a civilized, old maidish group, whose genuine wit was incommunicable because it was so inturned. I gained so much from the group, and it was so much part of my life for so long, that I cannot easily stand away from it. I think we had a lot of laughter and interesting talk, but I think we were inevitably rather smug— more than justifiably sure that Jane Austen had been right in basing her insights upon the compass of three or four families.

I was, however, the rover of the group, more naturally sociable, finding communication with all I met not only easy but almost unavoidable. I thus lived a strange life—as one of a very tight little group, from which I suppose I received nothing that I had not known before I went to Oxford, save for the independence that we all had of being at last away from our families; and also as someone who knew a number of sets of people or individuals—some very well—quite outside the little group, and quite unlike it in background or concerns. Two or three of these I shall write something of, for I could not have met them had I not gone to Oxford. They altered my outlook quite considerably, and, I think, they are not un-representative of the changing Oxford of the early 'thirties.

I think I can safely say that, until I went to Oxford, I had never known anyone of working-class background. There had, of course, been my London promiscuous sexual encounters. Many of these had been with cockney working-class young men. But this life which had begun before I was sixteen was a world as separate from my daily life as were my dreams (I dreamt and do dream a lot). It was to be many years before I began happily to connect the two lives, and certainly Oxford was for me something quite apart from active sexual life. Apart from that, the only working-class people I had known were servants—and, given my family's near penury, these were not many. I had never known anyone well who came from north of the Home Counties; and, apart from one visit with my father to Scotland to revisit his boyhood home in Dumfriesshire, I had never penetrated into England north of Hampstead. I think this is literally true. The glory of Merton was that by the natural course of events, simply through casual encounters, and more still through shared tutorials, I found myself among a group of people whose backgrounds were in varying kinds what I had been brought up to call 'working class' and who came from various parts of the Midlands and North. I was so class-bound that I was not very class-conscious. Thus it came about that I knew these very agreeable and interesting men merely as my fellow history students, and only gradually realized that their backgrounds and assumptions were so entirely different from my own. It was the very best way that it could have come about and I am deeply grateful to Merton for it. Of course, after a time, out of this agreeable and interesting group, there emerged two who were more agreeable and much more interesting to me. I owe them both a lot.

The first was a very small Jewish man from the Midlands with very expressive eyes and an irony of approach which fitted well to my own. It was with him that I sat talking, first about the history we were studying together, and then about life in general, until my scout (a very paternal man) expressed great concern that each morning the ashes of my fire were still glowing because I had sat up so late. I think those night-long talks were some of the most pleasing things of my Oxford time (and they had to be for me to endure being awake after midnight, something that all my life I've avoided since so much of my childhood was made miserable by my family's habits of very late hours to which I was monstrously expected to adapt at a very early age). I do not remember what Norman's father worked at, although it was in a factory; but the family were good solid Labour people. I had for some years, through the influence of well-to-do socialist parents of school friends and of left-wing masters at Westminster, vaguely professed Labour views. It was only now when I listened to Norman that these acquired meaning. It wouldn't be true to say that he did not propagandize, but only in so far as he could not bear to see someone intelligent that he liked so totally ignorant of the life that he knew so well. I think that I too felt a need over and above communication to convince him of the reality of middle-class and London life of which he was equally ignorant. We presented our lives and our worlds to each other, however, always in an ironic and absurd light. It was probably the only way that either of us could have accepted the reality that lay below the exaggerations.

His scepticism about Oxford and his determination not to allow it to penetrate his Staffordshire Jewish self was complete. We used to go together to Labour Club meetings and took part in occasional demonstrations. But he felt and he conveyed to me that this was all a kind of playacting of the real thing as he knew it at home. And of course he was right. As a result, we had as often to leave the Labour Club meetings because of our uncontrollable giggles as we did the history lectures. In particular, I remember going from a lecture of Dora Russell's on her school because we had woven a fantasy throughout her speech that she was Mae West in disguise sabotaging the Labour movement. This contemptuous approach to under-graduate politics meant, of course, that I never knew the aspiring politicians and famous left-wing dons of my time. The most prominent of these dons was Dick Crossman. Judging by his arrogance and cultural myopia when I met him in later years, I did not lose as much in this as I did, in general, by my failure to meet famous Oxford figures. In two different vacations I visited Norman at his Bilston home. His family were all very small people like him and his parents were Orthodox Jews. This lent a certain exoticism for me to their very pleasant household. He and his brother and sister had enjoyed a greater education than their parents, to whom they were devoted, but their parents were both highly intelligent people. This gave to the exotic quality of the home a sense of familiarity also, for my father, whom I equally loved, was also a less educated man than I and also highly intelligent. The only thing, in fact, about Norman's family that fitted my stereotyped image of working-class life was that they lived in a council house. I emphasize this because once again I acquired a sense of a world totally different from my own without any debasing self-conscious sense of 'getting to know the workers'. I was simply making some new unusual friends whose loyalties were very stoutly declared for the working class. I was also seeing Bilston, Darlaston and Wednesbury as they were at the height of the Depression, and this was most educative of all.

In return Norman came to stay at the house of my very impoverished, extremely chi-chi Catholic brother Pat, who was at that time trying desperately to run a tea-room at Pevensey. He got on with my brother as well as, I hope, I got on with his family. And I think he may have learned something from that visit also. I have seen him only once since the war. But I was told recently that he concluded from my writings that I had not changed at all since Oxford. This I know to be absurd. Recently I saw him on television speaking on behalf of Manchester Labour City Council. He seemed to me not to have changed. This is probably equally absurd.

In my second year I got to know Denis. He always spoke as though he was a working-class boy; but his father was in fact, I believe, an Inspector of Education in Manchester. Yet I suppose that he and his brother were the first two university-educated boys in the family. Denis has remained a close friend. I owe to him a different widening of my outlook. He was conventionally and stoutly Labour and had the habitual irony of all my friends. But he had a very confident attitude towards society and his future. He meant to succeed and he did, becoming a very top civil servant. Although I had no confident ambition, he gave me the sense that men who meant to be at the top were not people with whom I could make no communication—a first step to my later greater social confidence. He was also a thoroughly assured heterosexual. Had I gone to

Christ Church, I think that with the numbers of South of England public schoolboys there, I should hever have made such friendships. I am again grateful to Merton.

But not all Merton men were Northern or Midlands working class. Next door to me and a year senior was Stuart, the very epitome of a Byronic public schoolboy. Tall, handsome, enormously charming, with a wide Oxford social range, an easy culture, he seemed to me a figure out of a book. But he proved to be a very kind and friendly senior. And I in turn, I think, a good neighbour when he returned on occasion late at night from what I thought of as a gilded Oxford, rather helplessly drunk. Perhaps it was this relationship, or perhaps it was his having some musical instrument, I think a mandolin, but I always saw him as Steerforth, which, despite Dickens's overt moral disapproval of his character, is for me a very high compliment indeed. I think that he wondered why I should lead such a mousy life and have such mousy friends, and he persuaded me into a smarter Merton set—first to act in *The Doctor's Dilemma* in the Merton Floats and then to be a member of an exclusive dining club, The Myrmidons, where we wore special violet evening coats and violet ties. The dinners were most agreeable and delicious. And, once again, I am grateful to him for this entry to what still seems to me a direct Victorian survival with its deliberate intention of intoxication, its witty drunken speeches and its patronizing chaffing of the scout who waited on us. It could have been Dickens once more—Pip and the Finches of the Grove. Perhaps it was for this reason that I never felt I quite made the grade in the smart Merton world for, if it was sophisticated, it was also determinedly manly in the old Regency sense of the word.

I came to another Oxford world of sophistication, by chance, because Peter Glenville, the theatrical producer, had rooms next to a friend of mine at Christ Church. He, too, urged me into a wider life, which meant the OUDS, where I played in Marlowe's *Dr Faustus*. But my greatest success was in a smoker to which Peter brought Ivor Novello and (against the OUDS rules) Gladys Cooper. Here I did a skit of a well known débutante (I think) who had played the heroine in *Faustus* with a coy song, 'I won't be kissed on the lips', and represented one of the deadly sins in a chorus. How 'nineties our views still were may be seen by the fact that I represented the sin by wearing flame-coloured pyjamas and carrying a madonna lily. I enjoyed all the OUDS life, including the Sunday breakfasts, very much, and through it went to a number of sophisticated parties at which my camp wit went down rather better than among the Myrmidons. As to the aura of wickedness that still hung round the OUDS from the 'twenties, it never seemed to me to go further than 'daring' talk and camp flirtation. From my background of London promiscuity, I thought it all rather absurd. But now I'm inclined to wonder. Despite my gay chatter, I did carry a governessy aura around with me at Oxford and, for all I know, as soon as I left the parties everyone may have relaxed and started to have it off.

Finally I owe a debt to another group of three men at Merton, very intelligent, public school, sophisticated and dissipated. They were a year after mine, and perhaps this is why—sign of things to come—their greatest friends were all the most intelligent girls from Somerville. The smart Christ Church set, for example, went on in the old way and knew no women undergraduates, only debs from London and the shires. My friendship with these young women was a very enjoyable aspect of my Oxford life. From Barbara I borrowed the clothes I wore in the smoker. With the assistance of Sally I dressed up as the stepmother of one of our friends and completely spoofed the middle-aged parents of another at a tea-party. I can remember now how, dressed in tweeds and looking, I imagine, rather masculine, I leant forward to the conventional middle-class father and, cutting out his wife, said, 'You and I are rather more up to date, aren't we? We can appreciate Cézanne.' And his gallant, flirtatious agreement.

I mention this absurd episode because based on it, I believe, has grown up the sort of legend that always overtakes fact. An

Oxford don's wife said to me recently, 'I hear you spent nearly all your time at Oxford dressed as a woman. What fun those days must have been.' Such is how legend overtakes the very simple original which I have tried to set down here—an original much too shy to be in the smart set anyway, despite my continuous amusing chatter, an original who was pleased enough when his name got once or twice into the *Cherwell*, but who, in the main, enjoyed an Oxford that might have been any other place that allowed one lots of time to do just what one wanted. I am a little surprised, looking back, however, that I didn't want to do rather more.

Robert Boothby (Magdalen, 1919–21).

Raymond Massey (Balliol, 1919–21) in an OUDS production, 1920.

John Betjeman, Esquire.

John Betjeman (Magdalen, 1925–28) caricatured in The Cherwell, *27 October 1928. In a previous issue it was said of him: 'He could be a poet if he took the trouble.'*

J.I.M. Stewart (Oriel, 1925–28) in his first year.

Angus Wilson (Merton, 1932–35).

Nigel Nicolson (Balliol, 1935–38) in the College Eight (second from right, back row). Seated, second from right, is R.C. Sherriff.

(Bodleian Library)

Grimond (Balliol, 1932–35), ex-editor of
e Isis, which later described his term of
ce: 'Day after day, dressed as Siegfried or
tan and fondling his lion cub, he would
k into the Isis office and give a twist to the
nifold rack on which the sub-editors were
stretched together. . .'

John Mortimer (Brasenose, 1940–43).

Nina Bawden (then Mabey) at Somerville
(sixth from right, back row). On her left is
Margaret Thatcher (then Roberts).

*Antonia Fraser (then Pakenham) on arrival at Lady Margaret Hall in October 1950
(sixth from left, back row).*

*Alan Coren (Wadham, 1957–60), left,
talking outside Schools, 1960.*

Martin Amis (Exeter, 1968–71).

Jo Grimond

Jo Grimond was born in 1913 in Scotland and was educated at Eton and Balliol College, where he took a first class degree in politics, philosophy and economics. He practised as a barrister until the war, when he served in the 2nd Fife and Forfar Yeomanry and on the staff of the 53rd Division. He has been Liberal MP for Orkney and Shetland since 1950 and was leader of the Liberal Party from 1956 to 1967, and again briefly in 1976. He has been a director of the Manchester Guardian *and* Evening News, *Rector of both Edinburgh University and Aberdeen University, Chancellor of the University of Kent, and Chubb Fellow of Yale. He is married to Laura, daughter of the late Sir Maurice and Lady Bonham-Carter (Baroness Asquith of Yarnbury).*

My first sight of Oxford was the row of gabled Victorian houses which decorated the road to Henley. I approached the sacred city to take a scholarship examination. To me it was indeed a sacred city. I experienced some emotions faintly like those which it is said Luther experienced when first seeing Rome. Part of the troubles of university education today, it seems to me, stems from the fact that the romantic excitement of universities has departed.

Everything about Oxford appeared new, interesting and unexpected. I remember the peculiar mixture of the couple of days or so I spent at Balliol: the austerity of the rooms with their greenish walls and iron bedsteads and, on the other hand, the extreme agreeableness of 'Sligger' Urquhart's hospitality. F. F. Urquhart, the first Roman Catholic to be made a Fellow since the Reformation, was then still Dean. He was a leading example of a type of don now rare and much missed. He lived not for promotion nor by writing articles or books, but for the students of Balliol. He had his favourites. But he spread through the college a feeling of good-will. He combined relaxation with authority—authority flowing not from discipline but from his personality and the standards of behaviour which he exemplified. Why he was called 'Sligger' is uncertain but unlike many nicknames, particularly those bandied about in the press, it was the common way of referring to him. I remember, too, reading Robert Louis Stevenson's essays, but of the examination I have no memory. However, I got a scholarship.

My expectations of Oxford when I went up there were high and on the whole were not disappointed. All this was perhaps rather strange: in many ways Eton must be the public school most like a university. Yet the change from school to university seemed to me vast.

My first impressions of Balliol were not mistaken, for it remained a curious mixture. Its discomforts were typical. The only baths were a steaming inferno presided over by a one-armed man of great charm when one got to know him, but at first sight reminiscent of one of the keepers of the Underworld. These baths were some hundred yards across country; so were the lavatories. The staircases were stone and perpendicular. As an ingenious torment the lights would stay on for only a short time. This time was insufficient for the older members of college to reach the attics. I am told that a distinguished German refugee of advanced age was frequently found in pitch darkness half-way up the stairs waiting for someone at the bottom to switch the light on again.

On the other hand, there was the blissful sense of freedom— the joy of having one's own rooms: two rooms, not one; and also there was the hospitality of the dons who lived in college— again, at the head of these was 'Sligger'. By that time he was an old man and ill, but his rooms were still open when he was in college to almost anyone who wished to call. There he sat, pale and silent; nevertheless, people still liked his company and however painful it might have been from time to time he at least gave the impression of being inexhaustibly keen to see undergraduates.

Roger Mynors, who later became Professor of Latin at both Cambridge and Oxford, was another who kept open house. Friendly, amused but firm, he was the archetype of the best dons.

The great difference which distinguished the style of teaching at Oxford from that I had known at school was the assumption that you were of course deeply interested in the subject taught; that you were capable of infinite comprehension and, indeed, of making a contribution to it. Along with this went a fairly stringent examination of any opinions which one put forward. The first pure draught of Oxford life came to me when I went to a tutorial with Humphrey Sumner. After it was over he thrust into my arms two tomes which, with his charming diffidence, he suggested I might find interesting to glance through. On closer examination they appeared to be a detailed study of the Russian railway system as it had affected their military dispositions on their Western frontier. Part of the volume was, I think, in French, and I rather believe that some of the footnotes were in Russian, but it never occurred to Humphrey that everyone was not as clever as he. Then there were tutorials on mediaeval history with Vivian Galbraith, who lived in rooms of startling austerity. It was rumoured that he steadfastly refused to teach any history after 1600, but up to that fatal date he was a very stimulating teacher, and extremely funny. Rocking gently on a chair said to have been inherited from Tout, he was a great favourite of my contemporaries.

Political philosophy was taught me by the admirably clear John Fulton, philosophy by Charles Morris, later Vice-Chancellor of Leeds University. As he rolled about like some stranded dolphin, I had for the first time the alarming experience of being asked what the words I used meant. This type of examination was the hallmark of Oxford philosophy. A. J. Ayer was teaching the new dogmas of logic positivism, but even among the older schools this meticulous examination of meaning, if not actual grammar, was endemic. In the hall of Corpus Professor Pritchard lectured on morals with stupendous contortion of mind. Not only did he have to go back to the very beginning of his endless paragraphs whenever the Corpus clock struck (I believe he eventually had it stopped from striking), but on one famous occasion, after making sixteen false starts on some proposition, he petrified a girl who was sitting in the back by announcing that either she could wind her watch or he would lecture. It was said that a distinguished rugger player who had never considered that he had a mind was rather startled by Pritchard crying out during one of his essays, 'Stop, stop, if you go on reading that stuff you will ruin your mind.'

Mr W. M. Allen, who taught me economics, was another new experience. He had a genius, also found in some other Oxford teachers, for attaching the most erudite meanings to any stumbling propostion which one put forward. This was immensely heartening. If one ventured some such remark as that prices depended upon supply and demand, Mr Allen would leap upon it with delighted surprise and expatiate upon the genius with which one had hit off one of the more complicated new theorems of the Austrian school.

It is easy to laugh at the word-splitting of philosophers or the incurable optimism of dedicated dons, but there is no doubt in my mind that they were the making of Oxford. I wonder if they exist to the same extent in the modern university?

'Excellence,' the universities chant; 'centres of excellence,' they proclaim, demanding ever more money from an un-sympathetic world. To me Oxford was indeed excellent. The jargon of 'elitism' had not been invented—the word being reserved chiefly to describe very non-elite cafés. The excellence subsisted not in the labs, splendid as these may have been, nor in the buildings (some of breath-taking beauty, some hideous, most of them uncomfortable), nor in the amounts spent or the number of earnest committees earnestly manned. Excellence subsisted first of all, in the quality of the dons; and then in the enormous variety of opportunities open to the student. I had begun to hear about Atheism and Communism (which in those days were mildly unorthodox); I listened to queer psychological doctrines expounded by Professor Soddy; I was stimulated by the OUDS; and above all I was exposed to all those traditional

Oxford conversations that go on almost all night. I learnt from my contemporaries.

On my staircase were Jasper Ridley, killed, alas, in the war, the most brilliant of us, with a mind like a beautiful Clapham Junction through which ideas slid off at every sort of tangent, and Norman O. Brown, later to achieve fame as the author of *Life against Death*. I lunched off repulsive dishes with Ridley and Con O'Neill, then, believe it or not, even more pessimistic than he was in middle life and already with a major resignation to his credit. I find my contemporaries exceedingly difficult to write about. Jasper and Guy Branch were killed when very young, so no list of achievements is possible. Nor indeed would it be appropriate: their genius lay in being rather than doing. The expectation of seeing them was infinitely agreeable. Jasper was an excellent companion, equable, critical, eccentric, and materially undemanding. He was ahead of his time in suggesting the possible beauty of shaven heads—though he recommended them for some girls as well as for some film stars. Guy was also generous, eccentric and always in a good temper. His eccentricity took a slightly more flamboyant form, his sociability was more orthodox, running to parties and expeditions of all sorts. We were, I think, much more interested in people than are modern students. We discussed the inmates of the university, the hunger marches, the Spanish War, Baldwin (whom we rather admired) and Great Philosophical or Political Questions, on which people read papers to clubs.

The sort of excellence which Oxford dispensed depended on a two-way traffic. We actually *liked* the university. We were charmed into ecstasy to have so much provided for us; we did not yearn to organize the kitchen; we *enjoyed* dining with Tom Boase, the Dean of Hertford, or eating crumpets in the JCR and drinking beer in the buttery. We did not yearn to be premature civil servants engrossed in tedious administration and sabbatical jobs. I edited *Isis* for a term. I did it very badly (unlike Tony Woozley and Stuart Daniel and Paul Dehn, who

edited *Cherwell* and did it brilliantly—the exploits of Porno-
grapha Lady Purple-Passage were much funnier than anything
now in *Punch*). In those days we did it in bits and pieces,
between lectures and tutorials. Now I suppose all the staff
would be taking a sabbatical year and would require a budget
and a university printing works.

I was interested in politics, but I was never a member of the
Union. Over this I have no regrets. To have attended its
debates I would have had to give up something else. It is
absurd to generalize about the effects of the Union—its great
figures have been of many types. But it could—I put it no
higher—encourage that view of politics which expresses itself
in clichés suitable for speeches or articles. It has been a little
responsible for the superficiality of much political comment,
the sneering, the desire to appear to be on the inside and
claim a spurious intimacy with political figures even if you
have never exchanged a word with them. On the other hand,
some of the best House of Commons performers in the traditional style—Lord Boyd Carpenter and Sir Derek Walker-
Smith—no doubt owed something to it, though I suspect their
native abilities and training at the Bar contributed more.

There is no point in creating expensive universities unless
those who go there enjoy them, unless the interplay between
dons and students goes on all the time. A university is not like
big business or the army. In my day 'career structure' was a
name unknown. No Fellow of a college cried himself to sleep
because he was not a Professor. In St Andrews, where I was
brought up, Professor D'Arcy Thompson sailed through the
sacred town in an enormous billowing gown for over sixty
years. He presented me with a stuffed hawk when I was six.
That's how Professors ought to behave. But now when the
siren blows the poor wretches scurry off to complete their
endless articles on more and more abstruse subjects, or to sit
on the joint inter-departmental committee on the control of

mice in the gymnasium. I notice it is often the products of Oxford and Cambridge—those wicked haunts of elitism—who give up their evenings (and their pocket money and their wives' time) to entertaining their pupils, thereby showing an admirable social conscience.

What difference did Oxford make to me? What warts or dew did it leave upon me? There was a certain amount of rubbing-off. This influence seems to me underestimated in the innumerable reminiscences of Oxford figures, though I would not say now that to go to Oxford or Cambridge was an experience not to be missed. For that matter I would not say that to go to a university at all was essential to the good life. I nearly joined a firm instead of going to Oxford which would have despatched me to Buenos Aires. I wonder what then would have happened. I do not know. But I can make certain guesses.

The university of Oxford—and for that matter those of Cambridge and Glasgow and Edinburgh and, less certainly, Birmingham and Manchester—turns the thoughts of its students away from industry and commerce. No doubt many of those who haunt the plushier buildings of London's City and the neighbourhood of Charlotte Square in Edinburgh have university degrees, but the climate of our universities—especially Oxford—encourages rather commitment to the professions, or what is somewhat peculiarly called 'public service'. The 'rub-off' is in that direction, and it has done the country much harm. The richest and the most expensively-educated of my generation certainly did not grapple with problems of production.

I do not mean that more students from my day should have studied engineering (though they probably should) or business management or brewing, baking or candlestick-making. I do not mean that Oxford deliberately taught them that these were ignoble arts. On the contrary, all intellectuals deeply revere navvies. But that is just the difficulty. Intellectuals revere *navvies*, not entrepreneurs to engage them in new and useful enterprises. And it is reverence—not a desire to participate—which moves intellectuals. Professor Pritchard generously assumed that the rugger player had a mind, and was willing to expend great gobbets of his time and intellect in grappling with that intractable opponent. Should he not have said, 'How excellent you are as an athletic, simple, shrewd man. Do not attempt the higher reaches of philosophy. Production, action, expression, are far more important'? Better still, should he not have asked several of his Firsts in Greats to go out and bend their talents to industry or trade? After expending their abilities in their business during the day, they could have devoted their evenings to high thinking. And that thinking should have included how industry, economics, politics and morals were to be blended. As it has turned out there has been little or no blending. The thinkers have been speakers and publicists, not doers.

The universities have largely failed to live up to their name. The point of combining diverse subjects in one institution is to get those who practise them to discuss the universality of knowledge, of human experience, of the human situation. Specialized research into medicine or engineering or law should be carried out in separate and specialist institutions. That is what happened in the seventeenth and eighteenth centuries in England, when there were only two universities, and both were commonly judged to be sunk in sloth and ignorance. Yet it was the golden age of English science. The greatest of English historians, Gibbon, never read History. There was no such School. The great English lawyers did not learn their law at Oxford and Cambridge. Today the French Grandes Ecoles make one wonder if universities are necessary. The justification for universities must be that they offer a fully-rounded education. They should be breeding grounds for something better than bureaucrats devoted to the narrow claims of their particular subject. They should teach science and technology against the background of morals. They should care for the future and cherish the past. From the universities should flow an informed public, capable of judgement, and with some notion of the common good.

This goes far beyond not only science or medicine, but the mere study of philosophies or language or history or sociology or economics. Greats and Modern Greats at Oxford, and the Humanities in the Scottish universities, were the schools which came nearest to teaching the methods of *civilization*. Yet efforts to introduce something like Greats or Modern Greats into the new universities have not been a success. Nor has there been any greater understanding of science by non-scientists. I believe much of this is due to the Faculty/Department tradition, which has not really been changed by the introduction of Schools. For Schools too, though they may increase the number of subjects taught in each division, still emphasize the division of learning, still depend upon the old organization of the university into compartments.

What we need is not a dilution of effort by having, for instance, a first year in which several subjects are studied superficially. On the contrary, every student should have his mental capacities stretched and sharpened by being made to study seriously one of those subjects which can properly be called disciplines, such as medicine, the established sciences, Greek, or philosophy. But the university should also insist on a general training in what, for want of a better description, I will call moral philosophy. This should include some history of civilization and institutions, some teaching of general morals, some introduction to the presuppositions of law, politics and economics, and some acquaintance with European literature.

The Oxford of my day did not provide this type of education within the curriculum, but the college system went some way to correct this. The denizens of a college to some extent educated each other by exploring together the freedom which the university offered them. The luckier among them were in and out of each other's and dons' rooms talking of many things beside the subject in hand. Innumerable societies existed, as they still do. But, of course, the great difference between the

Oxford of the 'thirties and today was not only that it was truly collegiate—the colleges being much more than hostels in which we ate and slept—but that it was part of a different world.

Universities are sometimes said to be ivory towers but this is at best only a quarter true. The good-humoured complaint in my day was that the dons were always in the potteries lecturing for the Workers' Educational Association. As I have said, hunger marches, the Spanish War, strikes up at Heading-ton, the activities of the Oxford City Council, kept many dons and undergraduates involved in other people's affairs—more involved perhaps than today. No students, as far as I know, went to fight in Vietnam.

The Oxford of Tom Tower and Peckwater, of the Radcliffe Camera and the Codrington Library: the Oxford of punts on the Cherwell, blossom, carols from Magdalen Tower and crumpets in Magdalen rooms on a misty autumn evening with deer among the fallen leaves of the park—these are the Oxfords of nostalgia. They evoke careless, unhurried days. Certainly one or two such memories remain: an expedition to a pub on the Thames below Wittenham Clumps; a drive through the summer night to Suffolk in which the countryside seemed a reincarnation of Keats's England—eglantine, vast elms, deep hedges and villages of white-washed houses where farm workers drank beer outside the pubs. But the background to Oxford was work. Though I never learnt to apply my mind, or for that matter my pen or my eyes, for long, my conscience drummed away at me none the less, and I was sufficiently ambitious to mind what class I got.

Much of Oxford was depressing. Certainly in those days before John Betjeman had come into my life the beauties of North Oxford or of Victorian Gothic were not to me apparent. Even now my rapture for them is modified. I have always believed that universities should be in the middle of towns so that I cannot complain too much about the suburbs—but these in any case were off-set by the bustling and to me heart-raising clamour of Elliston and Cavell's and St Aldate's. Over Oxford life too hung the clouds that shadow any life; Oxford, too, had its share of dissatisfaction and boredom; of foggy afternoons with a smell of cabbage cooking.

After two years living in college I went into digs in Beaumont Street with Jasper Ridley, Mark Pilkington, Lionel Brett, and John Pope-Hennessy, and later in South Eaton Place with William Douglas-Home. I was lucky in my digs: they were agreeable, faded, comfortable, unexacting places where we gave small dinner parties and were admirably looked after. For all the convenience of life in college, most people who could find it—and afford it—preferred an unpretentious house outside. A room in such a house seems to me the ideal way to spend a year or two, but, alas, such houses are now difficult to find, expensive to keep up and depend upon a race of house-keepers which no longer exists.

If Oxford was independence compared with school, Beaumont Street was independence within Oxford. I suppose there were rules but I have forgotten what they were. As Finals were drawing near I spent much time in the Codrington and Radcliffe Camera libraries—and very irksome it was. But Beaumont Street was a base to which I would return with the same companions, with pleasure.

Oxford was the centre of our world during term. I went to London to eat dinners in the Middle Temple, but London was not the magnet it appears to have been to previous and sub-sequent generations. We went to few parties and fewer dances. Girls came occasionally, and female undergraduates aroused excitement from time to time when they appeared at lectures or the occasional meal. Academic dress becomes nearly all girls, and their value was increased by their compara-tive rarity. But during term we lived largely in a male society. And even in the holidays expeditions were seldom mixed—indeed, it would have been thought scandalous by most of our

relations. These expeditions in ancient cars bought for a few
pounds or borrowed from parents must be counted part of
Oxford. They were nearly the best part. I remember Zarauz
and Madrid, the terrifying, empty, scorched plains of Spain,
more vividly than much of Oxford blurred in Thames fog. I
went to the famous chalet of 'Sligger' Urquhart above Saint-
Gervais and below Mont Blanc. I found myself with Con
O'Neill in Germany on the night of the long knives when
Hitler carried out his first publicized murders. We gave a
young man a lift who insisted on lying hidden under our
coats in the back of the car and asked to be let out when we
got near to the French Border so that he could cross unseen.
We were inclined to laugh at him but when we were well into
France we were overtaken by the French police who searched
our car from top to bottom for no apparent reason. Perhaps he
was someone of importance in danger after all.

Another expedition started from Cliveden with David Astor
and Adam von Trott, and ended in Vinagradoff's rooms in
the old *Guardian* building in Manchester where he was Foreign
Editor—the first time I was ever in it. In particular, I remember
the lift, crowded as usual with the restless inhabitants of a
newspaper office, a peculiar hazard to von Trott who had
contracted a boil on a vulnerable spot.

I mention these matters, unimportant as they may seem,
because my more vivid memories are eccentrically trivial
rather than significant, and certainly not flamboyant. The
parents of my friends were more flamboyant than we were.
When William Home and I went to dine with one of his elderly
Lambton cousins we were dressed in unobtrusive dinner jackets,
he in a suit of crimson velvet. Sober we were (or, if drunk, not
often; drink for my contemporaries has been a middle-aged
vice), concerned about life and philosophy and literature and
death. Death figured quite largely. It seems strange now to
have suffered a pang on realizing that 'of my three score years
and ten' not 'twenty' but actually twenty-one would not come
again. Forty-nine to go seemed very few.

Beauty and Oxford are oddly conjoined. It has beautiful buildings but it is not as beautiful a place as Cambridge, nor as grand. Art, music and literature were admired and their appreciation encouraged. It would be wrong, therefore, to accuse the universities of being unaesthetic, yet of late they have put up some spectacularly ugly buildings. Nor do I remember any great awareness of beauty in most Oxford rooms—either of dons or students. Looking back, it seems odd that artistic effort was so infrequent. Some of my contemporaries played instruments, a few painted. The urge to create seemed weak. Why should it have been otherwise? Scholarship does not imply creativity.

> '*Bald heads forgetful of their sins*
> *Old, learned, respectable bald heads*
> *Edit and annotate the lines*
> *That young men tossing on their beds*
> *Rhymed out in love's despair*
> *To flatter beauty's ignorant ear.*'

I look back on Oxford with pleasure, yes, but with no great desire to repeat the whole experience. Its education was excellent. It certainly formed and stretched whatever minds were open to it. But perhaps the education was unreal. All education, of course, is unreal, in that boys and girls are rarely taught the skills of life: to type or mend a motor car, to cook or read a balance sheet. There are few more unreal places than those gorgeously-equipped laboratories in our schools where girls are taught to cook and boys to work at wood with tools they will never see the like of again. But the unreality of Oxford lay in the gap between the world of humanities taught there and the values of the world in which we lived. No one proposed that we should behave like the Greeks yet their philosophy and poetry were displayed for our admiration. Economics were remote from ordinary decisions—indeed the very dons who taught economics and advised governments did not appear to think that governments should act according to the rules. I am not saying that Keynes and Henderson, Hayek and Pigou did not have an effect on official thinking. No doubt too, Greek discipline enabled lawyers and administrators to marshal and deploy a case with economy and elegance. But the way of life was largely unaffected. Now we could perhaps do with some assertion of Greek values and pure economics, indeed, as I have mentioned, of theology and moral philosophy. We discover, however, that endless hours spent in memorizing Horace, passing examinations in the 'General Theory', going to chapel or discussing the views of Pritchard, Joseph, Collingwood or Joachim (all professors in my time), have left hardly a mark behind. The efforts to bring the benefits of Oxford to a wider public, the WEA and Ruskin College seem to have led to no great flowering through the nation of the spirit of reason and the wide view; nor indeed to any great improvement in our critical faculties or values. It may be that it was the education for a ruling class which has hung on miraculously well but is passing. At any rate, of its sort it was good.

Nigel Nicolson

Nigel Nicolson was born in 1917, the younger son of Harold Nicolson and Victoria Sackville-West. He was educated at Eton and Balliol College, where he took a third class degree in History in 1938. He served with the Grenadier Guards in the African and Italian campaigns in the Second World War. In 1947 he co-founded the publishing firm of Weidenfeld & Nicolson with George (now Lord) Weidenfeld, and he is still a director. He was Conservative MP for Bournemouth East from 1952 to 1959. He has written a number of books, including Portrait of a Marriage *(1973). He has edited his father's diaries and letters, and also the letters of Virginia Woolf. He lives at Sissinghurst Castle in Kent.*

The school chapter in an autobiography can by tradition be a pretty gloomy record, but by the time the hero reaches university, he is expected to show by selective anecdote and deft allusion to names which subsequently became famous, that he was at last in the swim, and that the university meant for him a sudden flowering of talents and lifelong influences and friends. For me such deception would be outrageous. I made a mess of Oxford, and Oxford did not make much of me. My three years (1935–38) began in disillusionment, continued in despondency, ended in a third class degree in History, and left not a single intimacy and little affection behind. I write this confession in order to exorcise a memory, and to explain to myself how it happened.

It was not Oxford's fault. My present ingratitude is caused entirely by wasted opportunity. Where you do not succeed, you cannot love. Periodically I return to Balliol, pace its quads, climb my old staircase, and each glimpse of a scarcely-altered scene reminds me of humiliation and idleness. 'He was unhappy at Oxford.' Not quite true. There were moments of exhilaration when I felt myself sharing, if not generating, triumph—on the river, at the Union, late at night. But these moments were rare. More often I retreated hurt, disconsolate and envious, for a university is the period when envy takes precedence of admiration, and self-approbation alternates unpleasantly with self-distrust. My dominant mood was depression, but I was damned if I was going to confess it. I have re-read for the first time the letters I wrote to my parents during those years. Even at this distance of time I know that they conveyed a deliberately false impression. I made the most of small successes, magnified acquaintance into friendship, and exaggerated the frequency, length and stimulus of undergraduate discussions, describing an atmosphere of youthful abandon, and concealing my melancholy and loneliness. How often did I sit miserably by a miserable fire, hitting with a poker at the coals, and hearing distant shouts of friend to friend, and the banging of doors that signified my exclusion.

It was parental expectation that led to this deceit. My father too had been at Balliol. Throughout his life, as he wrote in old age, the name of Oxford, even on a pot of marmalade, quickened his pulses. He had found there a sudden release of energy and spirit, discovered the joys of literature and friendship. Surely it must be the same with his son? Balliol, he told me, was a palimpsest of achievement on which every generation writes its new chapter. To him it was still the Balliol of the early 1900s, and before that of Jowett and Curzon. There was a tradition of disdainful pride, of effortless superiority. The rest of the university, we were led to believe, envied us. We were the centre, with the highest standards, the greatest charm, the most Firsts. Captivated by this legend, even I would answer when asked for the name of my college, 'As a matter of fact, I'm at Balliol.' But outward pride was not matched by inner confidence, and privately I wondered where the magic was of which my father had so often spoken. Had it really been so glamorous in his day? Did he never endure pangs of indolence and inadequacy? Was he not recreating a myth?

I have found the letter which he wrote to me on the eve of my first term:

> 'The main thing to remember is that it is half a school and half not a school. In other words, you cannot treat it

exactly like a hotel, and yet you need not treat it as a Summer Fields boy would treat Eton when he goes up for a viva. ... Balliol does not care overmuch for the extent of a man's knowledge: it cares dreadfully for his state of mind. They would far rather that you were ignorant than that you were silly. If you do not know something, and say so, they will not care in the least. But if you pretend to know something which you do not know, they will care very much indeed. Remember that what they want to find out is whether you are *intelligent*, not whether you are *learned*. They judge intelligence by the extent to which you avoid saying something stupid rather than by the extent to which you manage to say something bright.'

Now that was all very well. So anxious was I not to say anything stupid, that I never said anything at all. I was desperately shy, and shyness at nineteen may be a pathetic quality, but it is not particularly endearing. On arrival I found an invitation to lunch with a senior Fellow, Roger Mynors. I knocked on his door with the sort of knock that tries to be casual, but only succeeds in conveying timidity. He greeted me affably, even warmly, but I noticed a quick glance at my eyes for some indication of intelligence, and my heart sank. My fellow-guests were the two Pope-Hennessy brothers, John and James, both undergraduates, but with social and intellectual gifts that soared beyond my own. The conversation soon turned to Piero della Francesca, of whom I had heard, just, but could think of nothing to add to John's amazing flow of erudition and analysis. James took all this in his stride, poking his brother's fire with caustic comment, while I sat silent. Eventually Mynors turned to me.

'What have you been reading lately?'

'*Emma*.'

There was a slight quickening of interest. 'And what did you think of *Emma*?'

'Rather snobbish,' I said.

They resumed their discussion of Italian art.

I knew the right note to strike, but not how to strike it. I found the attitude of the dons, half-masters, half-colleagues, intimidating. They were living symbols of that glorious past. A row of baits was dangled before me, but I spat them out. At school there had been insistence that one be in certain places at certain times to carry out definite tasks. At Balliol nobody seemed to care what one did. In other people, I observed, this sudden freedom led rapidly to conceit. We were being treated as adults. The mere fact that the crudities of converse at school were succeeded by the politeness of university intercourse persuaded them to identify that politeness with admiration. It was so startling to find 'Oh my God, Nicolson' replaced by 'Hullo, Nigel, have a drink', that it was tempting to attribute the alteration in manner to some hitherto undiscovered prowess in oneself. An assumption of disapproval became overnight an assumption of approval, and to many the change was intoxicating. But not to me. It was as if water-wings had suddenly been snatched away, and I was afloat unsupported at the deep end. My efforts to adopt the Balliol manner were floundering and embarrassing. I had never known time go so slowly. After two days it seemed that I had been there a fortnight. I felt myself to be under constant scrutiny, and that opinions were being formed about me which were unflattering, irrevocable and true. Panic seized me. I allowed something of it to leak into my letters home, and in a rare burst of confidence, recorded this verbatim conversation with my tutor Humphrey Sumner:

H.S. (sharply the whole time): 'You were at Eton?'

N.N. 'Yes.'

H.S. 'Where did you spend your last holidays?'

N.N. 'At Tours.'

H.S. 'Nice place. Where did you go when your parents were in Persia?' (He seemed to know all about me.)

N.N. 'I stayed with my uncle in Devonshire.'

H.S. 'Nice uncle?'

N.N. 'Not too bad.'

Really, I felt, this is absurd, and rather cruel. But what was Sumner doing except fishing for an interest, a character, a peg on which to hang something? He was a difficult, admirable man. Tall, wiry, pipe-smoking, he had a prodigious capacity for work, and set his pupils unattainable standards—his own. He distrusted generalization, and disliked epigram. He elicited opinion, but seldom expressed one. Once he asked me, after I had read an essay on Napoleon, 'Do you like Napoleon?'

'Quite,' I said.

'I hate Napoleon.' There was a dead silence: at last he had committed himself. His unsolicited answer became famous, and so, momentarily, did I. I was the man to whom Humphrey had said that he hated Napoleon. His austerity was strange and frightening. He asked his pupils to call on him whenever they wished, and a fortnight later I did so.

'Have you come to talk about something special,' he asked me, looking up from his work, 'or just to talk?'

'Just to talk.'

'What about?'

I could not catch this ball. It required an experience beyond me, and after a few unproductive remarks, I shambled out, self-confidence lowered by several more degrees. For all his kindness, he was a terrifying man. There seemed to be nothing that he did not know. We tested it; it became a game. A friend of mine, with an impertinence I envied, was marooned in Bergen for a few days, and spent his time learning all he could about Norwegian football teams, with the sole purpose of confronting Humphrey with knowledge that Humphrey could not possibly possess. On returning to Oxford he worked the conversation round, with some difficulty, to his newly-acquired speciality. He began by touching lightly on the tactics and prospects of Lillehammer and Trondheim, only to find himself immediately challenged. Humphrey was conversant with every statistic, the name of every star player. After that, we never tried again.

With so much discouragement under the guise of encouragement, so much freedom, such an excess of opportunity, I grew lazy, which I had never been at school, and spent hours staring out of the window at the St Giles traffic, bustling importantly to the library to find unnecessary quotations or through the Junior Common Room looking right and left as if in search of someone with whom I had an appointment, but only hoping to be hailed. It was weeks before I discovered where the bathrooms were (steamy catacombs where no bathrooms should be), being too shy, and as time passed, too ashamed, to ask. I sat in hall, always in the same place, scarcely speaking to my neighbours, and they began to look curiously at me, for I seemed, alone among my contemporaries, to have no fun, and not to desire it. Do I exaggerate my loneliness? I do not think so; and I believe that my experience was, and perhaps is, far more common than undergraduates dare admit. One needed psychological counsellors, but Balliol was too proud to provide them. After all, the place, in the most civilized way, was highly competitive, and you had to learn for yourself to use its tools. I experienced no unkindness, no form of ostracism, but simply mounting despair. How untrue it is that memory retains the pleasures of life, to the exclusion of its pains!

That was the first year. The second was better. It was impossible that things should not improve for someone who, after all, was not a natural misanthrope. I slowly made friends. One was a jolly Portuguese, Peter Bon de Sousa Pernes, who teased me out of my moroseness; another was Rohan Butler, who gallantly fought down the handicap of a painful stammer, and with him I engaged in earnest discussions, but he was a cleverer man than I was, a potential, and later an actual, Fellow of All Souls, and our friendship was not destined to last. A third, and the most important, was James Pope-Hennessy. I owed more to him than to anyone else, don or undergraduate, for he took me by the scruff of the neck, declaring my solemnity absurd, and forced me to bicycle with him through Normandy one long vacation. I think that was the turning-point. I learnt to laugh with him, to quarrel and forgive, to enjoy excess, and he taught me that in nine cases out of ten a person dislikes you only because he imagines that you dislike him. James seemed made for Balliol, with his cleverness, companionableness and charm, his slenderness, black hair, and willowy walk, but he was one of the few among us who did not last the course. He left Oxford after two years, without taking a degree. He thought the place stuffy. There was the occasion when a delegation waited on him (it now seems incredible) to complain that his gaudy ties were giving the college a bad name. There was his essay on constitutional innovations in the reign of Queen Elizabeth, which turned out to be a discussion of the Queen's personality in terms of her dress, starting with her slippers and mounting to her jewelled hair. He was told to do it again, properly. Although he remained throughout his life boyishly irresponsible, he was already too mature for Oxford. While I found it too free, he found it too restricting. His departure was a terrible blow to me, but his example left much behind.

Stars circulated in our small firmament, a few young men who embodied all the qualities which I recognized to be central to Oxford's purpose, and I knew some of them peripherally. The most brilliant constellation was formed of three who were killed in the war—Jasper Ridley (we called him 'Bubbles', a singularly inappropriate childhood nickname which he had never managed to shake off), Guy Branch and David Wallace—and three who survived to attain the eminence expected of them—Stuart Hampshire, John Pope-Hennessy and Jeremy Hutchinson. The centre of their élitist group was 7 Beaumont Street, lodgings which I later occupied myself with less galactic companions. When allowed to, I sat literally at their feet, on the floor. Ridley, discovering me there for the first time, leant down to ask, 'What do you think of Tuesdays?' a question which today I might manage to laugh off, but which then crushed me into silence. Branch was kinder. Two years older than me, he had been my hero at school, and still was, and in an attempt to break down this most inhibiting of all relationships, he took me to his room, which was furnished and carpeted entirely in white, with the first white telephone I ever saw, and told me how unhappy he had been when he first came up to Oxford. I don't think I believed him.

Women were lacking from our lives. Of course we knew that they were around, but somewhere in the outer suburbs, convents loosely linked to our great monastery, but unvisited, and from which no visitors came. In all those years I never once entered a women's college, and never knew a single girl well enough to call her by her first name. Perhaps, even for Balliol, I was exceptional in this, but I do not think so. We took our cue from the dons, who discouraged heterosexual love, it now seems to me, as irrelevant to our purpose in being there, and treated girls as blue-stockings who could not be expected to understand our male society. There was a don at Hertford whose course of lectures on Edward II I was advised to attend. About fifty of us assembled for his first lecture, including six girls. He looked down the hall, wrapped his gown protectively around him like a toga, and declared: 'I do not lecture to *undergraduettes*' (the word was expelled with mordant sarcasm, heavily italicized). 'I will not begin until they have left the room.' Spontaneously we all rose and walked out. Next week we returned, including the girls, and he surrendered. Now this may seem in retrospect a splendid demonstration of university solidarity, but it was more a gesture of romantic chivalry on which we greatly flattered ourselves, and a noble excuse for avoiding a lecture which we expected to be dull. None of us ever spoke to the girls whose champions we had so unexpectedly become. There were no Zuleikas among them. In fact, in the whole university there was only one who could lay even approximate claim to that title, and she was a White Russian. She was called Tatiana Voronoff. Ignoring the taboos which the women's colleges accepted as their sad lot, Voronoff thrust herself into our monastic world, filling our rooms with heavy scent and sexy Caucasian-Parisian laughter. There must have been some who loved her, for she was very beautiful, but in most of us she confirmed an incomprehensible prejudice. She had heavy artificial eyelashes, apparently dipped in tar, and was much rouged. She wore fluttering silks. Her long white fingers were ringed in amethyst, and tapered to lacquered nails. I hated her.

Such were my glimpses into unattainable worlds. So was the world of politics. Once I spoke in a Union debate, late at night; and once with Niall Macdermot I attempted to organize a university branch of the National Labour party, and we invited down from London a leading member of the party, Kenneth Lindsay, to address our inaugural meeting. Four people came. On that terrible evening I realized, not for the first time, that I did not possess the charismatic gift. Nor did I recognize it in others, for which there was little excuse, since among my Balliol contemporaries were Edward Heath and Denis Healey. I knew both of them slightly, but ask me to describe them as they then were, and I find the focusing difficult: too many later impressions have supervened. Of Healey I recall his gift for mimicry and comic ballads, and his rubicund amiability, but nothing of the ruthless courage with which he is credited today. Heath is sharper: his way of laughing until his whole body shook, his undeviating gaze, a touch of puritanism, and his passion for music, for he was our Organ Scholar. But when he became President of the Union he swam out of my reach. I was not yet deeply interested in politics. The Spanish War was for me little more than a serial story in the newspapers: the Hitler crises—although I spent two holidays with anti-Nazi families in Berlin and Göttingen—recurrent excitements. I would like to claim despair, or at least apprehension, at what was about to happen to my generation, but I cannot. We did not want war—particularly as the most agreeable Rhodes Scholars were German—but the thought of it did not appal us. It would rouse us from lethargy, we thought, and make us short-cut heroes, while the idea of an early melodramatic martyrdom nurtured our self-esteem. There were no pacifists among my friends, except one, Douglas Young, a formidable Greek scholar, stiffly bearded like a youth on an Attic vase, and saintly in his gentleness and humour. We called him God, and when required to act the word 'dog' in a word-game, we carried him into the room upside down.

The upshot was that there was no group into which I naturally slotted, and that was distressing for someone so desperately anxious to slot. So I took to rowing, hoping that the unison of an eight would link me to at least some of my fellows, as in a chain-gang. It worked. I much enjoyed rowing. The Balliol eight was drawn from all parts of the college, including two Americans and a Canadian as cox, and we were good enough to be awarded our oars one summer, and to row at Henley. The companionship was pleasant, and so was the exercise, for the rhythm of a well-trained crew has no parallel except perhaps in dancing, and the implements of our sport were as beautiful as its river setting, eight identical oars cupping the water simultaneously each side of a long light shell in which we perched and slid, floating forwards, lunging back, in silence except for the rumbling of the slides and the piping injunctions of the cox. I spent happy hours on the Isis, but the best was Henley. There we were in competition with the finest crews of several nationalities, and at no moment in my life have I experienced so *sustained* a wish to excel. For those few days we lived in dread of the next race, discussing tactics, grooming the boat, eating enormously, sleeping long—and then the last terrified backward glance at the course before the race began in distant privacy to end ten minutes later between banks of parasols and tumultuous acclaim. Those were ecstatic moments.

But work? Surely I worked? Yes, in spasms timed to the climax of the weekly essay, and the less thought I had given to it, the lengthier were my last-minute plagiarisms. This was the temptation of easy access to great libraries where one could find obscure books which even Humphrey Sumner might not have read, but he always had. I worked, but I did not study. I would take up an eighteenth-century novel with the excuse that it gave me 'period-feel' when I should have been acquiring solid information or digging deep enough into a subject to reach its subsoils and justify me in differing from a scholar's opinions. To lose time at Oxford was good: to waste it was a crime, and I wasted all too much of it. I would take on holiday to Venice Stubbs's *Constitutional Charters*. Stubbs remained unread, but Venice was ruined by his reproachful presence. There were days, however, when I felt myself gripping something, and I associate them mainly with the Codrington Library at All Souls, the loveliest, coolest room in Oxford, to which I was given privileged entrance. The long hall was almost empty except for book-filled shelves, but alcoves sheltered us, and we read in silence. There was no escape, except in humiliation. Having paced the length of that marble floor, one could not decently retreat along it until many hours had lapsed. Under pressure of confinement, I began to learn what study is, the joy of documents, the mean pleasure of finding experts wrong, and to form, gradually and inter-mittently, an attitude of my own. Then I could test it against Sumner's pouncing mind, argue my point-of-view, and feel the muscularity of his response.

Too late. I sat my final examination with apprehension, memorizing each night my past essays in the hope that the same subjects would recur, learning by rote quotations which might fit in somewhere (oh, the shame of it), and then scribble, scribble in the Examination Schools, gowned and bent, envious of neighbouring scribblers, twisting questions to admit pre-pared answers, trying to deceive but knowing all the while that deception of this kind is always detectable, as it was.

I aimed for a Second. I achieved a Third. The news reached me in Glasgow. I was on my way to the Outer Hebrides to spend a fortnight on some uninhabited islands which I had just bought with a small legacy, and I took with me Rohan Butler. It was the year of the International Glasgow Exhibition.

We decided to separate at the entrance, and meet again three hours later at a designated spot to compare impressions. When Rohan returned, he was carrying a copy of *The Times*. Casually I asked him if the Schools results had been published. He said they had.

'What did you get?' I asked.

'I got a First.'

'And what did I get?'

'You'd better look.'

I looked. I searched expectantly down the Seconds list, failed to find my name, and then the Thirds. It was there.

'Get in,' I said. We drove an hour in silence. Then he said, 'Do you realize that we're going the wrong way? We're driving south; it should be north.'

'Yes.' I reversed. Gradually the blood began to recirculate. I thought, 'Here is this man, my friend, in ecstasy. Here am I, his friend, in despair. Why should I spoil his pleasure?'

He was infinitely kind. We camped on my island, never mentioning the contrast that was in both our minds, and quarrelled only once, about forks. He insisted on civilized behaviour. I ate with my fingers from the tin.

That for me was the end of Oxford, for him almost the beginning, for he is still there. Oxford, I felt, had condemned me, and I deserved to be condemned. When I return there now, I may avoid Balliol because it has every reason to be indifferent to me, but with each visit I find things which I never bothered to discover as an undergraduate. Last summer I climbed to the cupola of the Sheldonian, looked across the pierced view and downwards onto flat roofs, and sighed to think how much I had missed, wishing myself nineteen again, but without reproach, except self-reproach. Now my son is nineteen. From shame, and because I hope to enjoy vicariously a new deal, I am sending him to Cambridge.

John Mortimer

J was at school when the war started, dark days for Europe and, I was finally convinced, for me. The bastions of freedom were falling, the lights going out all over the place, and we stood in the Speech Room singing the school songs, 'Five Hundred Faces and All So Strange', 'Jerry a poor little fag', those fiercely nostalgic evocations of Victorian boyhood. An ancient and quavering voice was added to ours, the sibilants slurred as from too much brandy or ill-fitting teeth. Mr Churchill, not yet Prime Minister, had come down in search of his distant youth. After the singing was over he was helped onto the platform and peered at us like a misty-eyed tortoise, his hand trembling on the ivory handle of his stick. He said a few words which I didn't find easy to hear or to understand. 'If they ever put *him* in charge,' I said to my friend Oliver, 'then we're all goners.' Shortly after that Mr Churchill took over the war and I went to Oxford. I was seventeen and had I not written poems about Spain at my prep school? Had I not been the sole occupant of a Communist cell at Harrow? I must surely be top of the Nazi black-list; and when they crossed the Channel they would inevitably make a bee-line for me.

I went to Oxford, therefore, in expectation of imminent death.

My going there at all was a late decision of my father's. Old,

blind and brilliant, his income had increased with the call-up
of younger barristers. 'I think we might run to Oxford,' he
said, 'provided you fall in and read Law.' I fell in, but after
Oxford what was to happen to me? My mind was continually
changing; should I become a pilot? Or even, and it seemed at
times the most courageous alternative, a pacifist? 'The best
place for you is the RAF groundstaff,' my father told me.
'Avoid the temptation to do anything heroic.'

I wondered why he chose Oxford. He'd been at Cambridge
himself and Brasenose was a college which he'd only heard
mentioned, in an apparently disparaging way, by someone in
his Chambers many years before. But as he offered me Oxford
like the sausage and scrambled eggs of the condemned man's
breakfast, I felt it churlish to refuse. I presented myself,
accordingly, for an entrance examination.

Whenever I hear now of the appalling efforts, suffering and
anxiety of those who are trying to get their children into the
older universities I think of my entrance examination with a
pang of guilt. I went to Brasenose and was led up some stairs
by a college servant. After a long solitary wait a bald-headed
man wearing carpet slippers and carrying a large dictionary of
gastronomy under his arm came shuffling in. He handed me a
passage from Lucretius, told me to translate it and shuffled
away. I sat for a while puzzled by the complicated stanzas
describing the nature of atoms and then another door opened.
Through it came my friend Oliver also carrying a book.
'There's a shop on the corner,' he said, 'and I went out and
bought this. I think it might be a help.' It was a Latin dictionary
and he had slipped out unnoticed and acquired it at Black-
wells. With its help we wrote out a translation and went to
find our examiner. He was having lunch, reading a recipe from
the book propped up on a stand in front of him whilst he
feasted on—what was it—dried egg, spam salad perhaps? He
took our work without a word and later we discovered we had

passed into Oxford. I never saw the bald gastronome or, indeed, very much of Brasenose College again. It was taken over by the War Office and they sent us to Christ Church.

Oxford after France fell, as the black-out was pinned up in the Buttery, as Frank Pakenham, history tutor at Christ Church, drilled dangerously with the Home Guard in the Meadows, was at the end of an era, and I was at the end of my extra-ordinarily secluded middle-class, 'thirties education. Although Harrow is a stop on the Metropolitan line we never used it except to sit, jeered at, dressed in a top hat, pearl-grey waist-coat and carrying a stick with a blue silk tassel, for our annual visit to Lords. We weren't allowed to speak to the boys at the bottom of the hill, although the Prefects occasionally gave one of them sixpence to carry a suitcase up at the beginning of term. The only women we saw were elderly and fierce matrons. We were waited on at table by footmen in blue tailed coats and settled down for the night by a butler called George. Our homosexuality was therefore dictated by necessity rather than choice. We were like a generation of diners condemned to cold cuts because the steak and kidney's 'off'.

I can't say I came out of this bizarre hothouse and met the real world at Oxford. That encounter, intoxicating, painful, invigorating, hilarious and tragic, was held from me for two years until, in the company of GI's, cameramen, electricians, aircraft workers with their Veronica Lake hairdos tied up in scarves, script girls and infantrymen, I stopped being educated and came, belatedly, to life. Meanwhile I lay becalmed at Oxford.

The Oxford of the 'twenties and 'thirties was still there, like college claret, but it was rationed, on coupons, and there was not very much of it left. The famous characters still behaved as if they lingered in the pages of *Decline and Fall*; indeed, they were famous for nothing except being Oxford characters: once they left their natural habitat in Magdalen or the House they grew faint and dim and ended up down back corridors in Bush House or as announcers in Radio Monte Carlo. They had double-barrelled names: Edward Faith-Peterson, Tommy Motte-Smith. By day they lay naked in their rooms listening to Charles Trenet or Verdi's *Requiem*. By night they would issue into the black-out, camel hair coats slung across their shoulders like German generals, bow ties from Hall's settled under their lightly-powdered chins, to take the exotic dinner (maximum spending allowed under the Ministry of Food Regulations— five shillings) at the George Restaurant. What did it matter if the steak was whale (Moby Dick and chips) or the wine rationed Algiers or even black-market Communion? They still talked about Beardsley and Firbank and *Point Counter Point* and how, sometime in the summer vacation, they had been spoken to by Brian Howard, supposed model for the Waugh heroes, itching in his A. C. Plonk's uniform in the downstairs bar at the Ritz.

So at Oxford after Dunkerque the fashion was to be queer. It seems that it was only after the war, with the return of the military, that heterosexuality came to be completely tolerated. As it was, my own sporadic adventures with WAAFs and girls from St Hilda's, my grandly-titled 'engagement' to a student of book illustration at the Slade, were subjects I preferred not to discuss with Tommy Motte-Smith when he invited me and my friend Oliver for whale steak at the George.

The high life of Oxford, of course, was something I had never encountered when I moved into my rooms in Meadow Buildings. To my dismay I found I was sharing them with Parsons, a tall man with bicycle clips and a pronounced Adam's apple who tried to lure me into the Bible Society. One night my friend Oliver and I tried the effect of boiling up Algerian wine, college sherry and a bottle of Bols he had stolen from his mother's dressing-case, in Parsons's electric kettle. Oliver's mother was an ageless South American who moved in an aura

of patchouli and poodles round a series of rented flats with
white wrought-iron furniture in the area of Charles Street.
Perhaps for this reason Oliver saw himself an an eighteenth-
century English squire and this extraordinary brew was meant
to be punch, or hot toddy, or whatever eighteenth-century
squires drank in the evenings. When I recovered from the
draught I found Parsons wearing cycle clips and kneeling over
me in prayer: I also heard from down the corridor Brahms's
Fourth Symphony like music from some remote paradise.

In fact, my memory of Oxford seems, looking back over a
vast distance, to consist almost entirely of Brahms's Fourth
Symphony, a piece of music of which I have become decreasing-
ly fond, as I have lost the taste for bow ties, Balkan Sobranie
cigarettes, and sherry and Bols boiled up in an electric kettle.
But that music came from the room of someone who really did
affect my life and of whom I still think with gratitude and
bewilderment, remembering his serene life and extraordinary
death.

My father, to whom I owe so much, never told me the
difference between right and wrong; now I think that's why I
remain so greatly in his debt. But Henry Winter, who slowly
and with enormous care sharpened a thorn needle with sand-
paper to play Brahms on his huge horned gramophone, became
a kind of yardstick, not of taste but of moral behaviour. He
had no doubt whatever about the war: he was against it. He
looked forward to the call-up, the refusal, the arguments with
the tribunals and the final consignment to Pentonville or the
Fire Service with amused calm. He read classics, I mean actually
read them. He would sit in a squeaking basket chair, smoking a
pipe and giving me his version of chunks of Homer and
Euripides which up to then I had been trained to regard as
almost insoluble crossword puzzles or grammarians' equations
with no recognizable human content. I was born of tone deaf
parents and, in the school songs, I was instructed to open and
shut my mouth soundlessly so that no emergent discord might
mar the occasion. Yet Winter slowly, painstakingly, introduced

me to music, and the pleasure I now take in it is due entirely to him.

Winter's rejection of violence, and what seemed to me the extraordinary gentle firmness of his moral stance, was no result of religious conviction. He was courageously sceptical, fearlessly agnostic, open and reasonable, with none of the tormented Christianity of my ex-room mate. Parsons had applied for a transfer after the desecration of his electric kettle and left me in solitary possession of a huge Gothic sitting-room and a bedroom the size of a waiting-room at St Pancras, with a chipped wash basin in which I kept a smoked salmon caught by my aunt in Devon and in defiance of rationing.

I suppose Oxford's greatest gift is friendship, for which there is all the time in the world. After Oxford there are love affairs, marriages, working relationships, manipulations, lifelong enemies: but even then, in rationed, blacked-out Oxford, there were limitless hours for talking, drinking, staying up all night, even going for walks (how many years is it since I went for a walk?) with a friend. Winter and I were emerging from the chrysalis of schoolboy homosexuality; and the girls we preferred were notably boyish. Veronica Lake rather than Betty Grable, and Katherine Hepburn in *Philadelphia Story* who, Frank Hauser told us, was the natural bridge into the heterosexual world. At first the girls we loved were tennis-playing virgins, posed, like Proust's androgynous heroines, forever unobtainable against a background of parks and carrying string bags full of Slazengers. There is nothing like sexual frustration to give warmth to friendship, which is why it flourishes in prisons, armies, on Arctic expeditions and did well in wartime in Oxford. Winter and I became inseparable, and when, as time went on, I began to do things without him, I felt, for a moment quite strongly, guilty twinges of infidelity.

I had the more time for friendship as I did find learning law enormously dull and spent as little time at it as possible. I have always held the view that law has no existence whatever until people become involved in it, and that knowing a great deal of it is a hindrance rather than a help to the advocate in Court. Nevertheless, to fulfil my bargain with my father I acquired a working knowledge of Roman law and after about a year I would have been able to manumit a slave, adopt an elderly senator or enter into a marriage by the ceremony of 'brass and scales', skills which I have never found of great service in the Uxbridge Magistrates Court. Roman law was taught by a mountainous grey man who, like the Royal Family, had changed a German name for an old English one, who peered at me through glasses thick as ginger beer bottles and who was forever veering away from Justinian's view of Riparian ownership to Catullus' celebration of oral sex, a change of course which I found very welcome. Returning to Oxford by train from a legal dinner, he mistook the carriage door for the lavatory and stepped heavily out into the black-out and onto the flying railway lines just outside Didcot. After his death I gave up Roman law.

Other subjects I found encased in a number of slim volumes: *Tort in a Nutshell*, *The Basic Real Property*, *All You Need to Know about Libel and Slander*. I read them listening to Winter's gramophone, or as we punted down the river and the ATS in the long grass on the bank whistled, 'Keep smiling throo, Just as you, Used to doo, Till the good times come again one sunny day'. If these were not good times I was deceived by never having known anything better.

Oxford acting was good in those two years; but the universities had not yet become the natural training ground for the West End Theatre. Michael Flanders, not only alive then but upright, handsome and walking, played Pirandello's *Henry IVth* and gave me an admiration for that play which survived almost thirty years and was only shattered by actually seeing it again. Frank Hauser, who sat in rooms in Christ Church decorated with fleur de lys so that he seemed to be ever awaiting the imminent arrival of Joan of Arc, played Noel Coward on the piano and talked endlessly of the bit players in old Hollywood movies. He directed plays I had never heard of by Strindberg and Jean-Jacques Bernard, productions which I can still see in my mind. Peter Brook, ignored by the OUDS, made a film of *Tristram Shandy* with Tommy Motte-Smith playing Sterne. I acted a series of minor Shakespearian villains, but I always enjoyed the parties and falling hopelessly in love with the ladies-in-waiting, more than the performance. Finally I was cast as Rosencrantz and stopped going to rehearsals.

The war was also a time for poetry, perhaps the last time when poems were widely read; before the popular verse market was captured by folk singers and pop groups. I tried to write modern ballads heavily influenced by Auden, and was very proud when one or two got into the *Cherwell*. Since those days I haven't attacked a poem and I hope poetry is for my old age, like brewing home-made wine and spending every day in the garden. John Heath-Stubbs was a remarkable poet and Sidney Keyes a war poet about to meet a war poet's appropriate death. When twilight fell over Peckwater, pale, dark-haired Michael Hamburger, moving through the shadows with a heavy but always gleeful despair, used to come and read me his superb translations of Rilke and Hoelderlin. He was also besotted by the tennis-playing girls and seemed in constant fear that one might surrender to him, thereby breaking the spell of Gothic gloom in which he moved so happily.

Winter was a year older than I and was about to face his Tribunal. There was a man named Charles Dimont, then a character of great eminence in the pacifist world, who would give Winter a lesson in how best to put his reluctance to kill people to a bench of ex-officers and patriotic magistrates. Winter told me that a favourite question was, 'What would you do if you saw a German raping your grandmother?', to which

he intended to reply, 'Wait until he'd finished and then bury
the dear old lady again.' We went to Boars Hill, where Charles
Dimont lived, by bus. When we got there he had a bad cold
and was in a dressing-gown; there seemed to be a large number
of small children about, one of whom was dropping jam onto
The Bible Designed to be Read as Literature. In the corner was a
dark-haired woman of remarkable beauty who said nothing
and looked as if she was heartily sick of the tramp of bright
young conscies through her sitting-room. Charles Dimont
told Winter that it was very difficult to persuade the Tribunal
that you really didn't like killing people unless you believed in
God. He offered us a cup of tea, but the pot was empty and
anyway we had to go.

As we waited at the bus stop I had no idea that Charles
Dimont was about to change his mind and obtain an infantry
commission. I had still less idea that in some distant peace I
would marry the dark, silent Mrs Dimont and bring up those
numerous children, but that, in fact, is how it turned out.
About one thing, however, I was certain. I was going to take
my father's advice and sign on for the RAF groundstaff.

Star-struck by poets, Michael Hamburger and I used to travel
up to London. Drinking beer in the Swiss Pub in Soho we
might even be spoken to by Dylan Thomas or Roy Campbell.
When the pub shut we went to a terrible cellar called the
Coffee Ann where a huge Alsatian lay on a billiard table
chewing the ivory balls: over the loo a verse was pinned which
read: 'It's no use standing on the seat, the bloody crabs can
jump ten feet'. One drunken lunch-time Dylan Thomas, telling
us he was searching for a girl with an aperture as small as a
mouse's ear-hole, led us to the offices of *Horizon* where Stephen
Spender and Cyril Connolly, large as life, were sitting drinking
tea with a girl wearing wooden, hinged utility shoes.

Later I went to visit Winter in the Pacifist Service Unit he
had been sent to in Paddington. He never rebuked me for my

election of the RAF groundstaff, was duly impressed by my having met Stephen Spender, although I had had to hurry from the tea-table to dispose of the quarts of brown ale we had drunk at lunch-time, and told me that he had decided when the war was over to become a doctor. He was working as a hospital orderly and the fact that he would, as a classical scholar, have to start from scratch with elementary science, disturbed him not at all. I noticed that the Pacifists quarrelled violently about whose turn it was to do the cooking, and even about the size of their portions of vegetable pie. Only Winter remained imperturbably calm. After supper we played 'The Brahms Fourth' again: and Winter told me he had fallen in love with a girl whose head emerged from a cigarette kiosk on Paddington Station. He planned, as soon as possible, to get to know the bottom half of her. When I returned to Oxford it had become, I thought, rather dull.

I did my best. I went to the Slade School (evacuated to the Ashmolean), I sat in the life class before large nude ladies who were pink on the side nearest the radiator and blue and goose-pimpled on the other. I tried to draw them. Occasionally the teacher, a small grey-haired man in a bow tie, smelling faintly of Haig and Haig, would come, sit beside me, do a perfect drawing of the radiator side and leave without comment. I met a girl at the Slade and we became 'engaged'. She was very gentle, very quiet, came from Wales. I took her and her mother out to dinner at the George and, overcome with excitement and too much Algerian wine, seized a silk-stockinged leg to fondle under the table. I looked up to see the mother was glowering at me over the dried egg omelette: I had chosen the wrong leg.

My engagement, like my enthusiasm for Oxford, wilted. I had been for a medical and was rejected, even for the RAF groundstaff: but Jack Beddington, son of a barrister my father knew, was in charge of films at the Ministry of Information.

Mr Beddington, many years before, had seen me do *Charley's Aunt* in my puppet theatre and I had apparently just the talent needed to help film the defeat of Fascism. I got a war degree in the shortest time available. It was given with no ceremony. and, luckily for me, there were no classes. It was just one utility B.A. A degree in a nutshell. I left Oxford station for the last time and went up the line to London, scene of all excitement, the Blitz and the Swiss Pub, the Coffee Ann and the book shops in Charing Cross Road, Winter's Pacifist Unit in Paddington, the Ministry of Information with the silver barrage balloons in the blue sky, long trips with cameramen and electricians, leaving to write dialogue and scenes about a war which wouldn't stay still to be photographed. I was away a long time, but now I go there often; because my son's at Oxford, with the time, and the talent, to do it all properly.

Michael Hamburger became a distinguished poet as well as a translator of the German Romantics. Peter Brook did a thousand times more for the theatre than the Oxford theatre did for him. Frank Hauser stayed at Oxford and gave it plays to enlighten and stimulate generations of undergraduates. My friend Oliver joined a Guards regiment, fell in love with the Regimental Sergeant Major and was asked to leave. Later he married one of his mother's friends and went to live in Portugal.

And Winter? Henry Winter took his science exams after the war and became a country doctor, with a practice in the West Country. From time to time, when I wanted to know the difference between right and wrong, I would visit him and drive with him on his visits. In the evening we would drink beer and listen to Brahms and wonder what had happened to everyone we knew at Oxford.

I went to see him less and less and then one day he called on me in London. He had fallen desperately in love with a married hospital cleaner and wanted my professional advice about a divorce from his wife. What happened next I only read about in the papers. The hospital cleaner refused to live with him, they quarrelled and he killed her with a shot gun. He drove his car into a wood and swallowed most of the drugs in his medical case. It was some while before they found his body.

I think about it so often and still I cannot explain it. All I can suggest is that Henry Winter suffered terribly from not having taken part in the violence which was waiting for us at the age we went to Oxford.

Nina Bawden

In 1943, Oxford was a university restored by war to a strange and timeless silence. By edict, no bells rang and there was almost no traffic; the uncluttered curve of the High, the spires and towers of the colleges, slept in the clean, moist, quiet air as in some old don's dream of peace. After three years as an evacuee in the dusty confines of a Welsh mining valley and a final school term spent dodging flying bombs and sleeping in sandbagged shelters in London, I felt I had arrived in Arcadia.

I went to Somerville for my interview wearing my grammar school uniform; navy gym slip, red blazer, and hat. Two girls were already waiting outside the Principal's study, talking in high, neighing, upper-class accents. The pitch of their voices and a kind of expensive glossiness about their hair and their skin made them seem like healthy young mares. As soon as I heard them and saw them I knew it had been presumptuous folly to imagine I might be allowed to join this exclusive society. I told myself I should have known that the educational ladder I had climbed so laboriously would turn into a greasy pole as I reached the last rung. While the girls chattered breathlessly on I stared proudly ahead and smiled secretly. They went into the Principal's room one by one, and, when their interviews were over, clung to each other. 'Oh my *dear*,' they wailed, 'wasn't she *terrifying*. Of course we haven't an *earthly*.'

I was much more intimidated by them than by the prospect of meeting the gorgon who clearly lay in wait for me in the study. I knocked and went in. Helen Darbishire rose from her chair by the fire and held out both hands. She said, 'Come in, dear child. I have been so looking forward to meeting you.'

For a second I thought there must be someone else in the room for those two, superior girls to have been so alarmed, but there was only this small, rosy woman, beaming at me with a kind, grandmotherly air. We sat by the fire and she asked me about my family, my parents and brothers, and what I hoped to do 'after Oxford'. I said (timidly) that I wanted to write and (rather more confidently) that I intended to do something to make our country a better place to live in once the war ended. I told her about the people in Wales I had lived with; the unemployment in the valleys throughout the 'thirties, the miners with silicosis, the children with rickets. I feared as I spoke that my indignation sounded naive and affected but she listened with an interested expression as I unfolded my master plan to set the world to rights and, when I had finished, it seemed only polite to show interest in her in return. I asked what was her special subject? She told me her great love was Wordsworth. I said I had read him 'of course' but found him rather indigestible. Too wordy, I said, too sentimental. And all that romantic tosh about Nature! Helen Darbishire, the great Wordsworth scholar, heard me out patiently. She said I should try reading him again in a year or so and I might find I felt differently: the age at which one 'came to' a poet was very important. She smiled and gave me a chocolate. She said, 'Dear child, we will be happy to have you and I believe you will be happy with us.'

The *tone* of that interview is what I remember most clearly from Oxford; a sweet note of courteous respect for one's callow opinions, followed by a gentle suggestion that one might, perhaps, think again. This slyly effective educational method takes time and, in that fifth year of war, there was time in abundance. There were so few undergraduates and, proportionately, so many dons. I was taught mostly in single tutorials and, to begin with, found this concentrated exposure alarming. Enid Starkie, with whom I read French for two terms, was less tolerant than Helen Darbishire. I read her a long, pompous essay on Baudelaire. She looked at me with her astonishing eyes, like blue fire, and said, 'Nina, tell me. Do you know anything *at all* about sex?' Then, when I changed schools to read Modern Greats, I was sent to Lord Lindsay, the Master of Balliol, to be taught Philosophy. This was meant as an honour for me but it turned out a dismaying experience for both of us. He had not taught girls before and could not believe I had never learned Greek. He seemed convinced (although he was too polite ever to say so) that I must be concealing this simple and fundamental skill out of some mysterious modesty. He was very kind, comforted me with hot, milky drinks, and tried to explain about Bishop Berkeley. Unfortunately, what was so simple to him, the flowing order and clarity of his beautiful arguments, became, as it dripped through the sieve of my ignorance, bewilderingly muddled and murky. I began to feel as if I stood on the threshold of a brightly-lit room but a locked door barred my entry. I went to Helen Darbishire and asked if I might change my tutor. I said I was too stupid for Lindsay. She laughed and kissed me and sent me to Dr MacKinnon of Keble, a large, untidy, engaging man who rolled on the floor and played with the coal in the scuttle, sometimes chewing a lump (with frustration, presumably) while I read him my essays.

One evening he said, when I finished, 'What you have said is profoundly true. . . .' I waited, holding my breath—had the door opened at last without my perceiving it? The fire hissed. He sighed and shook his heavy head. '. . . And profoundly unilluminating.' I said I was sorry. He offered me a sardine sandwich with his coaly fingers and I was brave enough to explain about the locked door. He gave a relieved shout of laughter. 'All you need is a key!' He suggested a pupil of his, a young don from Glasgow who taught me, very slowly and patiently, the basic words, the first principles; coaxing me into the sea of philosophical method as one might coax and encourage a nervous swimmer until one day I realized, with detached surprise, that although I was out of my depth, my head was safe above water. . . .

Ungrateful memory cannot supply that kind young don's name, nor the names of others who taught me. Only faces, voices, remain. There were two refugee European Professors. One wrapped me in a rug (Oxford, in wartime, in winter, was damply, bone-achingly cold) while he read Hobbes aloud in a Viennese accent, or flirted with me, saying I reminded him of a squirrel. 'You are so shy on the ground but once safe in the tree you chatter and chatter.' The other, a whey-faced giant with large, dangling limbs that seemed only loosely tethered to his vast frame, tried to persuade me that darning his socks was a more suitable occupation for a young girl than learning statistics. And there was a small, gallant Englishman who had been dropped into France during the Resistance and occupied our tutorial hours very pleasantly by telling me how interesting (though alarming, of course) his experiences had been, and showing me how to light fires without kindling, using neatly-folded newspaper fans. I cannot remember what else he taught me, any more than I can remember the contents of the lectures I occasionally attended. All that comes back, try as I will, are small things. G. D. H. Cole's red carpet slippers. And Lord David Cecil's more neatly shod foot gyrating in circles, his sweet, elfin face wildly grimacing as he read a paper to a literary society I sometimes attended.

There were so many societies. Standing in front of the notice board my first term, I was dazzled by the delights that they all (with the exception of the Bell Ringers and the Rowing Club) seemed to offer. I had only to join this, or that, for a whole new world to open before me, a glittering world of agile and civilized argument, of brilliant occasions at which I would shine, and, most important of all, meet young men. I longed for young men in a way that was not consciously sexual, nor even romantic. At my girls' grammar school I had often felt isolated; been laughed at for 'odd' ideas and opinions. This had made me nervous of my own sex and a first look round my fellow pupils at Somerville had not suggested I would fare any better at Oxford. Like the girls at school they seemed to fall into two distinct groups: the plain ones, with their damp, eager smiles, drooping skirts and wrinkled stockings, and the beautiful and self-sufficient young goddesses who were already, while I eyed them cautiously in the early days of that term, greeting each other in hall and Common Room with confident affection and laughter. I did not want to be trapped by the first group and I feared that the second would never admit me to their exquisite company. Men, I told myself, would be easier to get on with, more tolerant, as well as being more interesting. Once I knew some young men everything else, the social and intellectual excitements I longed for, would automatically follow.

This approach had its pitfalls. By the time I discovered that some of the plain girls were amusing, not all the goddesses quite unapproachable, and that the ideas some of my school friends had found so extraordinary were almost distressingly common at Oxford, I had spent a great deal of time doing things that secretly bored me, like watching rugger, or drinking beer, or discussing Wittgenstein. I joined the Welsh Nationalist Society in pursuit of a Welshman; painted flats for an Experimental Theatre Club production of *The Dog Beneath The Skin* because I admired (alas, from afar) a second-year medical student at Magdalen. Although I had no real desire to join the Oxford Union (the standard of debate was so low, most of the speakers so deep in youthful self-love they made me feel old and tired as I listened) I threw pamphlets and balloons from the public gallery in support of a motion to admit women because the President invited me to. That was Tony Pickford who, with his frail, beaky good looks, his style and intelligence, seemed to me the only exemplar in the whole university of what I had expected Oxford to be; the fact that he was known to be suffering from a fatal disease gave him an added, and awesome, romantic attraction.

Tony was 'so mature' we said to each other at Somerville. Maturity was a quality we prized very highly because most of us so conspicuously lacked it. We had come straight from school, our call-up deferred; the sprinkling of undergraduates over nineteen were either, like poor, clever, doomed Tony, and later, Ken Tynan (clever but silly we dubbed *him* at Somerville), unfit for the services, or refugees from battle-torn Europe, or even older wars. There were several aristocratic and charming Chinese with whom I celebrated V.J. night in London, one of whom claimed to have walked out of China across the Indian frontier 'disguised as a peasant'.

Our war barely touched us. It was there, in the background, but we had grown up with it and were used to it, grumbling on over our heads like so much tiresome, adult conversation. In the vacations we worked on farms and in factories, and during the term we were detailed to help the war effort for a fixed number of hours a week, but since my particular duty was listed as 'Entertaining American soldiers' I found it no hardship. All I ever did for those polite, bewildered young men, kicking their heels in the camps outside Oxford, was to serve as a waitress at the Red Cross Club in Beaumont Street. Although I knew other girls did more—it was clear that one undergraduate, who changed from her drab working clothes into butterfly garments made from home-dyed cheese cloth when she left college at six every evening, was not just setting forth to cut sandwiches—an obscure prudishness stopped me admitting it. Fellow students gossiped and giggled. I maintained that if this particular girl was more generous with her time and her company than the rest of us, it was largely because she understood the Americans better. She was studying sixteenth century English literature and it was well known that the American language was closer to Shakespearian than to modern English. It wasn't only a matter of accent, but of the way words were used. When this argument was received with coarse laughter, I backed it up by quoting the Master of Balliol. His war work with our allies consisted of taking occasional Philosophy seminars and he had told me that he sometimes found communication difficult. A statement like, 'Well, I guess I swing along with Berkeley here,' was, he said, a fair example of how two nations could be divided by a common language.

We were divided by more than that. These Americans were new to war; pampered, peace-time children with smooth, milk-fed faces, whose fledgling innocence about the kind of minor privations we were accustomed to, amused, astonished, and shocked us. Working at the Red Cross Club, we were often appalled by the amount of delectable food left on plates and casually thrown away.

Not that we were ever really hungry. We were rationed to two ounces of butter a week but college meals were adequate if dull, and cheaply supplemented by British Restaurants, by the Taj Mahal in the Turl where you could get a good lentil curry for ninepence, and by the Cake Factory at the end of the Banbury Road. Since men and women were not allowed in each other's colleges before lunch or after six in the evening, tea was the meal to which we invited each other and the Factory cakes were standard fare. Wholesome enough to begin with, they went stale very rapidly, and there were girls at Somerville who claimed to measure the strength of their host's affections by the freshness of the buns he offered them. If they were still moist, he cared enough to have risen early and bicycled to the Factory before they had sold their supplies for that day. However much he protested his passion, if his cakes had already acquired that familiar, desiccated texture, disintegrating drily on the tongue, he could not be considered really 'serious'.

This kind of innocent, romantic conjecture occupied a great deal of our time and attention. Most of us were virgins, though we often affected not to be, out of pride, and we yearned for love. During the vacations we sometimes fire-watched in the

museums and libraries and, although I remember one eerily
unpleasant week, spent sleeping on a camp bed between a
mummy in a glass case and a stuffed alligator, what chiefly
comes back, when I recall the part I played in the defence of
my city, is sitting on the roof of the Bodleian Library playing
planchette with an upturned glass and a circle of letters, trying
to coax from the Fates the colour of my true love's hair.

I find I remember, not the important occasions, but the
unimportant, private ones. I remember V.E. night, the
tumbling bells, the joyful streets full of people, but chiefly
because I met an undergraduate at Carfax with whom I fell
in love. And although I can, with an effort, remember being
unhappy sometimes, crouched chilly and bored in my room
waiting for something exciting to happen, what I remember
with ease are the happy times. A dance at Queen's, wearing a
black taffeta dress I had bought second-hand; swimming
naked in the river with my great friend, Mairi MacInnes, the
poet; skating on Port Meadow when it flooded and froze one
bitter January; the mysterious, pale beauty of the blacked-out
colleges on clear, moonlit nights; evenings at the Playhouse,
or the Classic Cinema in Walton Street where they always,
invariably, seemed to be showing Hedy Lamarr in *L'Extase*. I
remember the pleasure of my small, dull, box-like room where,
for the first time, it seemed, I was able to be, or to become
anyway, the person I wanted to be without interference except
of a kind that only protected my freedom. I never found
college rules irksome. To have to be back in college by eleven-
fifteen was an excellent way of escaping, without appearing too
unsophisticated, from unwanted sexual entanglements. For
those who did not want to escape, there was a door into
Somerville from the Radcliffe Infirmary that was usually open
all night. If it was locked, for some unpredictable reason, there
was always the high wall between the college and Walton
Street. The only time I climbed it, I sat on the top and saw
Helen Darbishire walking in the garden. She looked up and
said, 'Who is that?' I was too frightened to answer. Helen had

always been gentle with me, but she was not gentle with everyone. Already that term, she had sent two girls down—for idleness, I realized afterwards, but at the time I believed it was for climbing in after hours. But all she said was, 'Oh, it's only you, Nina. Do get down at once, child, and have a hot bath before going to bed. You might get a chill, sitting on that stone wall.'

My affection for Somerville is centred almost entirely on the small, warm, dignified person of Helen Darbishire. Beside her, other dons seemed remote and cold and I was never much involved in the internal affairs of the college. Among my contemporaries the ones I remember, apart from close friends, are those whose paths crossed mine later, or who have achieved some kind of fame. I remember Richard Burton partly for this obvious reason, but I would have remembered him anyway, for one strange, shared experience. He was an RAF cadet, up in my first year, on a two-term short course. He called at Somerville one afternoon to take me out to tea. He arrived, limping dramatically. He had cut his foot, he announced, and was in terrible pain. I was only moderately sympathetic, and it amused me to observe that his limp disappeared as we left college and walked to the tea shop. The shop was closed and we stood on the pavement, feeling hungry and cheated and looking, I imagine, disconsolate. A lady appeared from the house next door and said, 'Were you two young things wanting tea?' She was a small, bright, bony woman with an incisive, cultured voice. We smiled at her foolishly. She said, 'You poor dears, how disappointing. Will you let me give you tea?'

She swept us into her house, up to a first-floor drawing-room full of rich clutter: pictures and books and fine carpets. We sat where she told us, on a silk-covered sofa in front of the fire and eyed this grand room and each other awkwardly. She brought a huge, laden, silver tray and set it before us. She said she had to go out, to a lecture, but we could stay as long as we wanted, take our time over our tea, and just remember to close the front door firmly behind us when we had finished.

We were too amazed even to thank her—as I remember it, neither of us spoke a word. She vanished with a merry wave of her hand, a good fairy in this odd, Oxford pantomime; her heels clicked down the stairs, the door slammed. Richard said, 'Do you think she really belongs here? I mean, suppose she's the maid?' I said she wasn't a servant, you could tell by her accent; she was just kind, and eccentric. But his doubts set my mind working. The tea was delicious, the scones home made and thick with real butter. While Richard talked about the part he was playing in Nevill Coghill's production of *Measure for Measure*, I wondered if our generous hostess might be a madwoman, given to inviting strangers in from the highways and byways and feeding them the family rations. Or worse— a cunning, professional thief who had stolen a few priceless trinkets and was using us as a kind of camouflage screen, while she got safely away. Richard asked me if I would like to spend a weekend with him in London. He knew Emlyn Williams, he said, and we could stay at his flat. I shook my head, laughing nervously. Even if I had believed he knew Emlyn Williams— and I was sure I could recognize a boastful lie when I heard it —I would have been far too preoccupied to consider the offer seriously. As I ate greedily, I listened for the sound of a key in the door, a heavy step on the stair. Any minute now some large, angry man would burst in, accuse us of breaking and entering and telephone at once for the police. Of course they would realize we were innocent *finally*, but there would be a lot of unpleasantness first. And rightly so. We hadn't stolen any- thing, not intentionally, but we had eaten this tea—scones and jam and several ounces of butter. We would be humiliated, exposed as gluttons! I said I felt sick, and Richard agreed we should go. He seemed apprehensive himself suddenly, though his estimation of our hostess was more charitable than mine. He said, when we stood safe outside, 'She was very trusting, wasn't she? You'd have thought she'd be worried we'd walk off with the silver.'

I may have met him once or twice after that but what rings
in my mind whenever I see that coarsely-pitted, middle-aged
rake's face on the screen, is that one, awed, boyish remark.
He is fixed in my memory at the age he was then as Margaret
Thatcher (then Margaret Roberts) is still a plump, neat,
solemn girl of nineteen. We came up the same term, both
grammar school girls on State scholarships. Our first year
college photograph shows us standing, side by side, in the
back row, but my only clear memory of her is, appropriately,
of a political argument. I was an active member of the Labour
Club and it astonished me that she should have chosen to
join the Conservatives. I told her so, one afternoon in Storm
Massoda's room. Storm had a cold and was sitting with her
head under a towel inhaling Friar's Balsam. Margaret and I
argued over her shrouded head. The world was changing, I
informed Margaret; to cling to the habit of deference towards
the 'top people' which was all, to my mind, she was doing by
belonging to the Conservative Club, was not only old-fashioned
but a clear dereliction of duty. She and I, with our lower
middle-class backgrounds, had been lucky to get into Oxford.
We should not use our good fortune simply to join the ranks of
the privileged but to make sure that when the war ended a
new, happier, more generous society would take the place of
the bad, old, selfish one. I cannot remember how she replied—
I was enjoying the sound of my own voice too much to listen
to hers—but sensing, perhaps, that my lofty sentiments were
not having quite the missionary effect I had hoped for, I
shifted my ground and pointed out that the Labour Club,
besides being on the side of the angels, was also more *fun*. All
the really lively and interesting people were members—Ernest
Gellner, Michael McMullan. Margaret smiled, her pretty
china doll's smile. Of course, she admitted, the Labour Club
was more *fashionable*—a deadly word that immediately reduced
my pretensions—but that in a way suited her purposes. Unlike
me, she was not 'playing' at politics. She meant to get into

Parliament and there was more chance of being 'noticed' in the Conservative Club, just because most of the members were a bit dull and stodgy.

Perhaps I felt, briefly, put down. (Storm, rearing her head from her towel, said, 'You lost that round, Nina.') But if some of us in the Labour Club were playing at politics, we were soon playing in earnest. The whole Labour movement was riding on a high tide of hope, preparing for the election of 1945. A contingent of us went to Reading to fight for Ian Mikardo and found ourselves caught up in an extraordinary atmosphere of political excitement that everyone seemed to share—soldiers on home leave, old men in pubs, tired women in bus queues. We canvassed until our feet were blistered and our throats were sore. We slept in the Labour Party Hall, ate marmalade sandwiches at the People's Pantry, marched through the streets singing, 'Vote, vote, vote for Mr Mikardo, chuck old Churchill in the sea.' We were hungry and happy and enthusiastic, convinced that the New Jerusalem was dawning.

When we came back after the summer for our last year the shadows were already lengthening. The war was over and Oxford was changing. The ex-servicemen were returning, the scholars first, under Class B release, and they seemed to our eyes to be older than their actual years warranted; stern, purposeful men with wives and moustaches, taking over our university and reducing us, by their middle-aged presence, to the status of schoolchildren. There were compensations, of course: more excitement, more people—among them, Tony Crosland, John Wain (who published my first short story in *Mandrake*), Henry Fairlie, John Watney, my cousin, Dr Cushing, returning to Balliol—but on the whole we felt displaced uneasy, slightly resentful. Our cafés, our streets, our societies— the whole of our playground was invaded by demobbed soldiers and sailors and airmen; colleges where we had previously known almost everyone were full of strangers; the Radcliffe Camera, so comfortably adequate for its reduced, wartime population was busy as a mainline station at rush hour.

Everything, and everyone, seemed so busy, suddenly. The feeling that one was special, and favoured, was fading; a feeling exemplified for me by the retirement of Helen Darbishire and the appointment of Janet Vaughan as Principal of Somerville. She was a good appointment, an excellent, worldly, efficient woman whom I respected, but I missed Helen's especial quality which was to make me feel loved and valued, not for anything I had done, or was likely to do, but for the person I was at that moment.

Most people feel their generation is unique. I think mine has a real claim to be. The austerity of war concealed social and financial differences. Since we were all poor and shabby, neither poverty nor shabbiness troubled us. Since we expected to be recruited into the services when we went down, we were not fretted by personal ambition. If we worked hard, it was for the fun of working, not to get our feet on the bottom rung of yet another ladder, and that is a rare kind of freedom. We inhabited, in a world at war, a peaceful, privileged oasis, and since in the vacations we worked as postmen or as land girls or in munition factories, we knew how privileged we were. But perhaps the most important thing is that we were so few. People had time, not just to teach us, but to welcome us. Oxford—*my* Oxford—has a distinct personality. When I look back I see, not spires, or sun-baked quads, or famous libraries, but a kind, clever old lady, holding out her hands and saying, 'Come in, dear child.'

Antonia Fraser

Lady Antonia Fraser was born Antonia Pakenham in 1932 and brought up in North Oxford. She went to the Dragon School, and later to St Mary's Convent, Ascot. She was up at Lady Margaret Hall from 1950 to 1953 and read History, in which she got a second class degree. She has since written a number of books, including Mary Queen of Scots, *which won the James Tait Black Memorial Prize in 1969, and* Cromwell Our Chief of Men (*1973*).

J see it all in terms of clothes. Which is odd, as I have not been much interested in clothes as such—more in myself inside them—ever since. Nor were any of us endowed with enough money to be really exotic in our dress. It was just that we were all so obsessed with authority and conformity, that our clothes were the only way we could find to indicate our submission to the former, our desire for the latter. No one had yet heard of a life-style, let alone acquiring furniture or learning cooking as a manner of self-expression. We more or less had to fall back upon clothes. As a result, you could at least tell not so much what people were but what they wanted to be from their appearance. The famous spires were way above our heads. Oxford in my day was a city of dreaming wardrobes.

Again, the desire for conformity was odd, because in 1950 clothes rationing had only just ended. You would think we might have broken out. Yet most men were dressed with a formality I am sure they have never since surpassed. William, for example, wore garments of a solemnity which would not have disgraced a Victorian Prime Minister: it is good to think that he subsequently found the right niche for his wardrobe as the editor of an august newspaper. At least such positive sartorial statements made things simple. Caroline, who was a Communist and most dashing, wore a shirt of solid red. Shirley, who was not a Communist, but was a prominent (now famous) member of the Labour Party, wore a shirt of checked red and white.

Theatrical people, whom I longed to know but was too frightened to approach, wore a great deal of black. The men seemed to have black hair to go with it; in fact a black polo-necked jersey, plus some black hair and eyes to match was an almost certain sign of the Experimental Theatre Club. Members of it appeared to be preoccupied in talk, sophisticated talk by the sound of it, and generally to have a great deal of fun. My lot were, alas, too nervous ever to get involved. Besides, we didn't have the right things to wear.

When I arrived at Oxford, aged just eighteen but already the veteran of the hat department in a Bond Street store, the accounts typing pool of an advertising agency, and a Do-it-yourself, Débutante attempt which failed, my own wardrobe was an amalgamation of all the compliments I had ever received in these varied situations. In particular it was dominated by a colour called Cyclamen Pink. This was because someone had once murmured aloud the name of my Revlon lipstick: Pink Plum Beautiful, and added romantically: 'Which goes for you too.'

That moment marked the demise of Midnight Blue as the prime favourite of my wardrobe. It had enjoyed a long reign— ever since, in fact, my best school friend Lucy and myself had agreed that Midnight Blue brought out the mysterious haunting brilliance of my eyes etc. etc. And of course I was ready to sacrifice Cyclamen Pink in a crime of passion of an instant, if anyone suggested it: I was always one to consider a wardrobe well lost for love.

However, no one was yet ready to accept the humble offering of my appearance. Therefore although the group photograph of Lady Margaret Hall first-year students is in black and white, I know perfectly well that my bat-wing jersey was of Cyclamen Pink. My black and white check skirt, on the other hand, came from Goray and had permanent stitched pleats, which were invaluable for bicycling.

Bicycling . . . It is extraordinary to contemplate an age when one did not have automatic recourse to Marks and Spencer, when cheap clothes were nasty clothes and served you right for being poor. An age without denim, above all an age without trousers. I well remember my first sight of a pair of blue jeans outside a Western film: they were worn deadly clean, rather wide, with neat white turn-ups. The girl who sported them, appropriately named Joy, was sitting on the handlebars of her boyfriend's bicycle, screaming with happiness as she whirled along. Of course one did see the occasional pair of trousers: the women of the Experimental Theatre Club tended to wear them, in black naturally, to match their men. Within Lady Margaret Hall itself they were generally worn late at night, or by those who wished to indicate that they were in an 'essay crisis': I sometimes found putting on a pair of trousers was a convenient substitute for actually getting down to write. But on the whole we tottered along on our bicycles, lower-calf skirts, stockings, suspenders and all. For this was the age of the stocking—I was still in theory darning my stockings at Oxford —an age before tights, before straight skirts, before mini-skirts. Everything we wore inevitably tangled in our bicycle wheels. I lived on a total allowance of £60 a year, which I could only make do by eliminating altogether all shop cleaning and shoe mending. Even today I cannot see oil marks without recalling those endless ravages of the bicycle to which all our wardrobes were subject.

The problem became particularly acute when it came to parties. In those days a party dress *was* a party dress, often of taffeta which needed a frilly petticoat underneath to sustain it: Lady Margaret Hall lurked at the end of Norham Gardens, a great red neo-Georgian dragon, ten minutes from public transport if you wore high heels, anyway my high heels, and that was infrequent. Taxis were beyond most people's means (although of course we did occasionally hire them as with many things beyond one's means). But the real answer was the bicycle. The truth was that our clothes, like ourselves, were romantic but hopelessly impractical for the lives we were supposed to lead.

The same air of unreality attended the love life of my particular circle. The rules of Lady Margaret Hall were strict and rumoured to be implacable: i.e. once you were caught breaking them, you would be put out. There were no late passes after midnight under any circumstances. You even needed permission to go to London; officially nights could never be spent away. No men were admitted to the college before lunch-time, and they had to leave by supper at seven. There were no locks on the doors. I was told that my Aunt Julia's generation at Somerville had been compelled to put the bed out in the corridor when entertaining a gentleman to tea. We did not exactly have to do that. But there was the same air of challenging restriction, obstacles which existed to be surmounted.

For of course we did surmount them. We all went to dances, came back at 2 am and climbed in by whatever the popular route of the moment might be. As our ball dresses were in the same high-flown style of our party clothes, it was fashionable to remove the dress first, before attempting the climb. Whether it was better to throw your dress over *first* and risk sticking on the wall, or count on your escort being able to lob it over afterwards to join you (and then the dress might stick) was the subject of much earnest theological discussion at breakfast. Shattering experiences were discussed. Later we all discovered that the easiest method was to sleep out altogether: in my case I hit on the expedient of returning for breakfast wearing a black veil, as though I had been to early Mass.

We were also wonderful at surmounting problems by assuming they did not exist. It was assumed, for example, that all my immediate circle lived in a state of perpetual virginity, which would not have disgraced St Ursula and her eleven thousand companions, because nothing, but nothing, ever terminated it. It was tacitly understood that one could survive the most delightful experiences untouched: perhaps we were like the

Aga Khan, on whose lips wine turned to water. At any rate what we firmly believed of ourselves, we naturally believed of our best friends. And this, despite all the evidence to the contrary which a life of lockless doors and endless spontaneous borrowing of other people's belongings (from Stenton's *Anglo-Saxon England* to Earl Grey's Tea) inevitably produced. Such incidents, such unplanned interruptions, were never discussed afterwards. Our talk amongst ourselves concentrated on love. We sometimes indicated gently that love might justify the ultimate sacrifice, that we might soon find it hard to refuse. But no one ever batted a cynical eyelid. We were the Romantic Generation.

If sexual experiences were theoretically minimal, social expectations were on the contrary great. Once there was a Drag Hunt Ball just outside Oxford, to which I had un-accountably failed to be asked. I asked God to do something about it, and God recklessly killed poor King George VI, as a result of which the Hunt Ball was cancelled. Not all social problems were solved so cataclysmically. Saturday night, for example. It was awful to be found dining in hall on Saturday night, because it obviously meant that no one had asked you out. Most of us preferred to heat up tinned Scotch broth in our rooms rather than face that. If caught, alone and in-explicably loitering, it was conventional to snatch up a book of poetry (Donne was rather smart) and indicate sudden world-weariness, a preference for *la vie intérieure*. . . .

The total lack of the telephone, and the existence of the college message service, brought a formality to social relation-ships which suited us very well. There were little notes of invitation, with initials in the corner, and there were occasional anonymous approaches ('I am the man who tweaked your gown impudently at the history lecture') as well as the equi-valent of the heavy breather. 'Dear Miss Pakenham, I could not help noticing in the Bodleian Library yesterday that we share a taste for German mediaeval bishoprics. This encourages me to suppose that we may have other tastes in common. . . .'

We all of us swore that we never accepted anonymous invitations, and this may in fact have been true as we all of us also lived in mortal fear of being seen out with anyone wearing a college-crested blazer, or worse still, a college scarf. Blazers without crests were esteemed patrician, but the college scarf rule was absolute, and none of us would have dreamt of breaking it. Thus missing, I have no doubt, the company of almost every interesting man then at Oxford.

As well as being pathetically (or anyway romantically) snobbish, we were of course frightful cadgers. There was no question of paying for one's own meal: they were the men, weren't they? Anyway, we were the young ladies. I think the only man who ever got me to pay anything for myself while I was at Oxford was my brother Thomas, whose time there happened to coincide with my own. And then it was only because he actually walked out of the restaurant, leaving rather more than half the bill at my disposal.

Anne was an immensely popular girl at Oxford, not especially pretty, but with a bright smile which worked wonders of free feeding. I remember one young man telling her bitterly when she was in her third year: 'Anne, you are made of food. Food paid for by other people.' Anne looked absolutely amazed, and temporarily even hurt, before philosophically helping herself to yet more asparagus out of season—we were at the Bear at Woodstock at the time. I certainly thought it the most bizarre remark: only subsequent reflection has told me how true it must have been.

At the time my own peach-fed appearance consisted of long brown curly hair and pink cheeks. I was also distinctly plump, or rather as I put it then and still prefer to put it now, rounded. It had not yet occurred to me that this particular appearance need not necessarily be accepted for the rest of time. It was possible, for example, to choose to be blonde, have short straight hair, and even be a good deal less plump. In my second year, these lessons began to come home to me. In general our appearances improved. Take Melissa, my Oxford best friend.

Melissa was small and sweet, a combination which was ravishingly popular. It also enabled her to overcome, most successfully, the rumour that she was incredibly clever. The rest of us putative scholars had to rely on our incredibly silly behaviour to give the unflattering story the lie.

On arrival at Lady Margaret Hall, Melissa was equipped with princess-line coats and princess-line dresses, made by her mother's dressmaker. I marked her down as a bit of a princess herself, not least when I noted her leaving for Morning Service at Christ Church in a fetching velours hat, presumably made by her mother's hatmaker. On these occasions Melissa was always much fêted, if not within the portals of the cathedral itself, at any rate immediately afterwards, and she never failed to secure at least three invitations to *post cathedra* sherry by Old Etonian members of the college (a coveted combination).

In spite of the influence of *Brideshead Revisited*, allegedly making Catholicism so elegantly desirable, there was no doubt that you got a much better class of invitation at Christ Church Cathedral of a Sunday morning than you did at the Roman Catholic Chaplaincy just opposite. My own attendances at this unremarkable building never resulted in anything better than invitations to go brass-rubbing or beagling from people who had been at school with my brother. And on one occasion I actually had to make do with an invitation *from* my brother (we would both share the costs of petrol to go and see John Betjeman, who was not however expecting us). Disillusioned, I abandoned the Chaplaincy and took to going to a short sharp Mass at St Benet's Hall in St Giles, where there were no rewards to be had, but no disappointments either.

Melissa's numerous admirers were easily marked out by their appearance. A Melissa Man possessed very long legs, encased in very tight cavalry twill trousers, cut quite as tightly indeed as denim now, but I think the objective was different, more *cherchez le cheval* than *cherchez la femme*. Anyway it must have been extremely convenient for bicycling. A Melissa Man had wonderfully thick hair, generally fair, on

which in colder weather he reverently placed a tweed cap,
the tweed however never by any chance matching the material
of his habitual tweed jacket. In really cold weather a Melissa
Man added a British warm overcoat. I was expected to mark
down Melissa Men, as hunters note the movements of rare
animals on the plains of Africa, but I was also expected to
keep off them myself. This was comparatively easy, because
few of them showed any signs of keeping on me.

For one thing, by my second year I had decided that my
style was Vivacious Gypsy. Cyclamen Pink was a thing of the
past, and I had acquired a red felt skirt, circular, terminated
by black braid; together with a V-necked black jersey (which
could be adjusted off the shoulders for quick changes), a black
elastic belt and black stiletto heels, this was a uniform which
saw me through every conceivable social occasion. I loved my
red skirt as a young squire loves his sword, and in order to save
it from the depredations of my bicycle, I even took to spending
special nights out, out of sheer affection for it. Also, as Nancy
Mitford's Lady Montdore believed in the sparkle of diamonds
round the ageing face, I now believed in the magnetism of
earrings. I had quite a collection. Indeed, had I been a pirate,
I would have dazzled the Spanish Main: I often lost one of
them on my way out to dinner on my bicycle. It would tinkle
down into the leafy gutter of Norham Gardens. I gallantly
rode on, wearing the survivor.

In our second year, things were on the move altogether.
Melissa was asked out by an Indian (what should she wear?)
and the Oxford University Conservative Club card had long
ago disappeared from her mantelpiece. The Oxford Labour
Club card had never stood much chance on mine: it was there
when I arrived, in honour I presume of my parents, both of
whom had stood in their time as Parliamentary Labour candidates for Oxford City. Like an unwelcome presentation
plant, my membership wilted and finally died. I certainly
never paid for it.

We did sometimes dine at the Union as guests: dinner

jackets for men, long dresses for girls. It was an admissible activity, so long as you were careful whom you went with. I once went with David, a licensed eccentric, but apparently his licence did not extend to taking me to the Union. My cousin Henrietta was the most tolerant person I knew, but it was in her other capacity as a remorseless observer of the social scene that she hissed at me: 'You made a great mistake being seen at the Union with David. Everyone says so.' I certainly wasted an evening. I cannot remember one word of the debate. Although it transpires by now that I was at Oxford with most of the leading politicians of our day, that whole side of life passed me by like a dream. Politics at Oxford was not at all what I had in mind. I had had quite enough at school of my father's unconventional Socialist views: 'A *Labour* minister?' someone would exclaim. 'Well, do you know this joke about the Labour government: They're like a bunch of bananas. First of all they're yellow.' Yes, I did know it. I'd heard it before.

By my third year I had got thin and fallen in love. It was lucky that the two processes coincided, otherwise it would have meant not one but two new wardrobes. I also discovered the pleasures of work—a subject, it will be noted, which has been singularly absent from this account: this, despite the fact that all the girls of my generation had to write two essays a week, in contrast to the men who only wrote one. Even with the minimal amount of study, this meant that our work must have taken up an enormous proportion of our time. The fact was that it did not take up the same proportion of our thoughts. Suddenly, in our final year, it was all different. We rediscovered that genuine scholarly enthusiasm which ages before had secured us those coveted places at Oxford. We felt again that pure love for history or literature which had once given rise to the rumour that we were incredibly clever. We regretted passionately that we had so long disproved the rumour by our incredibly silly behaviour.

It was of course rather late in the day for us foolish virgins (as we naturally still were) to trim our lamps. For three years

I shared tutorials with Carol, a wise virgin, who subsequently got the First she richly deserved. From the start her grim grey jerseys and baggy tweed skirts had indicated an insatiable appetite for work, which her behaviour had never belied. Now, at last, my friends and I found ourselves attired in the accoutrements of study. Jenny, my most beautiful friend, with the white face and red-gold hair of a Madonna, took to leaving make-up off altogether. As a result, she looked not so much earnest as consumptive. We were all much impressed by her appearance. Lipstick with us all became a rare occurrence. The object of my love was not at Oxford at all, and you could tell of his potential arrival on a Saturday evening by the fact that I donned a newly-suave corduroy dress of Forest Green— yes, Forest Green was in, its colour showing up the mysterious haunting brilliance of my complexion etc. etc. But I still wore earrings, a pair of dangling earrings with golden bells in them, giving a sparkle to the working face.

I thought a good deal about St Augustine, my favourite saint, and the fact that he too had been a bit of a late developer. How fortunate that I had learned from a novel by Ethel Mannin the correct translation of his famous words: 'Too late have I loved thee . . .'! Not so much too late as 'Late have I loved thee, oh beauty ever ancient, ever new, late have I loved thee'. I was most inspired by this text.

But of course, whatever the good luck of St Augustine, it was actually too late for me. Where our final exams were concerned, we were like very old people, who were nevertheless quite unprepared for death. Surely it couldn't happen to us? We didn't *feel* old. We were certainly not ready for death-by-examination. In fact, by June, the season of Schools, we were just getting into the stride of our work, enjoying it, making little discoveries, this after all was what it was all about, what we had come to Oxford *for*. . . . Why did no one ever tell us?

Too late. The date of the exams arrived. And suddenly the authorities imposed upon us, to our great surprise, something we had totally forgotten: a uniform! This was the so-called academic dress, the sub fusc or black and white clothing which was regulation wear for Schools. Men had to wear dark suits, white shirts and white ties. In girls, it took the equivalent form, black stockings, white shirts, black ties, black skirts. I had my fantasies about it. Sheer black nylons with seams, a white transparent nylon blouse with billowing sleeves, a floppy black velvet artist's bow as tie? It didn't work. The rules were strictly enforced. Ironically enough, it was in academic dress that for the first and last time at Oxford, I succeeded in what I suppose had always been my aim: looking exactly like everybody else.

Alan Coren

ħ ad I ever kept a diary, there is little doubt but that the entry for October 4, 1957, would have read very much like one of the hotter numbers of the *Anglo-Saxon Chronicle*.

It was that racy tabloid, you'll instantly recall, which first established the link between event and augury on a popular basis, thus laying the foundation for Great British Journalism. No fact was permitted to the record unless the editorial staff could relate it to fraught speculation of the most sensational and catchpenny order. Thus: 'This night, several comets were seen in the sky, and Bishops Aelforth, Aelwyth, Aelstryn all fell down foaming and died. Cattle went mad. A frog in Mercia ate a horse'.

It took the *Daily Mirror* nine hundred years to catch up. Yet even they, as a sift through the relevant file copy will show, did not notice that the moment at which I first alighted upon Oxford station, at 9 pm in the evening, was the exact same moment at which a far Soviet forefinger pressed a button to chuck the first earth satellite into brief orbit, ushering in, according to taste, either a new era of wonderful hope for all mankind or the end of the world.

Either way, it was good to be getting off the London train that day.

You felt somebody.

They were epochal days. Following the Suez triumph of a mere twelve months before, England basked in the high noon of Imperial magnificence. A new Elizabethan age had dawned, and nowhere was its mood more keenly felt than in Oxford itself. We had a radiant young queen—he had the room directly above mine, as a matter of fact—and, in Harold Macmillan, a Prime Minister who brought new meaning to undergraduate cabaret. Vivian Fuchs was belting towards the South Pole, Her Majesty Elizabeth II was rehearsing her very first televised Christmas message, Network Three leapt that winter from Auntie's fecund womb so that henceforth no undergraduate was forced to shave without the accompaniment of Pushkin, and, in general, it was a jolly good time to be British.

It is some indication of the depth and breadth of the general optimism that my only problem, that October, was an *embarras de richesse*. As the world was my oyster, so Oxford was my winkle: the question was, with which of my myriad pins should I attack it?

There was sport.

I had come from a rowing school. Situated as it was in lush council surroundings, School (as the jargon had it) lay no more than half a mile from Oaklands Park, that stretch of rolling chickweed which separates Foskett Bros (Grocers) Ltd from Standard Telephone & Cable, in verdant North London. Each summer afternoon, we day boys—the school being co-educational, many senior couples were given to spending the night in the bicycle shed—would stroll across to the park and buy such hours of boating as the fruits of our mugging would allow.

In consequence of this regular training, I became something of an oar, able quite often to keep both blades in the water simultaneously; and it was therefore only natural that my thoughts turned to the Oxford boat.

It was even more natural, after my first glimpse of the river, that they turned away again. There, in the chill fog, hundreds of young men paddled about in their underwear, their skin tripe-dimpled, their teeth leaving on the icy air the impression of a Flamenco eisteddfod. I, who had never touched oar without first buttoning my herringbone overcoat tightly about me, was shocked: no beer-crates cheered their skinny water-logged shells, no gramophones sang at their sterns, no busts broke the heaving vertical contours! This was not rowing as we that love the true sport know it.

I settled my smart rowing balaclava more snugly over my ears, and walked briskly away. And it was not long after that I determined to remain a stranger to all Oxford sport; for it was not in boating alone that the curious impositions of a cloistered other-worldly community had changed those games in which I was sparklingly proficient into weird unplayable mutants.

Football, to take a further example, was played with an ovoid, a shape calculated to knock out the eye of any centre-forward uncircumspect enough to attempt to head it, while tennis, though played in the correct manner (i.e. knocking the ball against a convenient wall), involved a tiny black pellet that flew back off the brickwork with such speed and incal-culability that the risk of having one's cigarette rammed down one's throat far outweighed any pleasure one might have taken in the game.

And as cricket was played by these suicidal eccentrics with a hard spherical rock which, if I'm any judge, would have torn the spade from one's hands and hurled its fragments all over the beach, I quickly abandoned all thought of a sporting career, and turned instead to the stage.

I suppose that neither before nor since that explosion of dramatic talent in the late 'fifties was Oxford as blessed with so dazzling an array of actors, directors, dramatists, and, above all, theorists of theatre. In the twin wakes left by the churning screws of Beckett and Osborne, literally hundreds of brilliant heads bobbed in the choppy water; that all have now sunk without trace points only to the cynical commercialism of the

West End theatre management clique whose bourgeois strangle-hold on taste ensures that profit, comprehensibility and pleasure are put before the challenges represented by thrilling experimentalists willing to transmute their nervous breakdowns into wonderful mimed symbolism or dramatize the Marxist view of the Black Death in gripping blank verse tetralogies.

Wadham, in those wonderful mould-breaking years, was the very cockpit of the struggle for expression. Young men whose names were on the tongue of everyone who cared about un-translated Rumanian allegory rightly eschewed the soft options of Shakespeare and Shaw in pursuit of their mission; which was to cull as many dramatic fragments as they could from the pages of very thin German literary magazines and stage them for the delectation of like-minded friends. Such was the dedication of these young producers to the concept of alienation, one would often see audiences running from their productions like field mice from a combine harvester.

This is not, of course, to say that the classical theatre was ignored: I myself sat through a powerful reading of *Charley's Aunt* in a freezing Walton Street hall, the object of which was to elicit the fundamental (yet until then unrevealed) conflict in the play between the heterosexual and homosexual elements in man's character. Spellbound, practically, I came to realize that Brandon Thomas had a message for all of us which, provided it was put across slowly enough, might very well change our entire view of what theatre was for.

As for the young lions who were actually writing original material, their myriad play-titles somehow escape me now, but I give the gist and temper when I say they were called things like *Waiting For Harris*, *Waiting For Rita*, *Waiting For Arthur*, *Waiting For Morrison* and so on, or else reflected the shrewd fancy of the time for Ionesco and Simpson and peopled the college stages with characters who believed themselves to be old beer bottles.

In short, it was a wonderful time to be alive, and encouraged by the general thespian frenzy, I threw myself into the world, nay, universe, of Oxford theatre. Michael Kustow, a Wadham colleague who later wrote a book in which he referred to himself throughout merely as K (a diffidence borrowed, with characteristic skill, to amuse those who knew and loved him) invited me to take part in a reading of *Chicken Soup With Barley*, one of the several thousand seminal masterpieces of the period. The production itself does not stick in the mind, but the preliminaries do; the cast had to lie on the floor of a cell in Somerville and perform a series of eurhythmic contortions which Mr Kustow had picked up from some Actors Studio manual of arms. After our reading from the shared Penguin, which was of course enormously enriched by the isometric vorspeise, I recall that Arnold Wesker sat rapt while Michael explained what the play was about. It was one of those precious moments when youth and age, innocence and experience, Academe and Life, theory and practice, suddenly all fused together into one lunatic whole.

After that, I auditioned for a major big-budget production of Aristophanes' *The Frogs*, designed, as I recall, to bring out both the Freudian undertones and the working-class *ur-politik* inherent in the original Greek. So great an impact did this audition make on the producer that I was immediately assigned the job of organizing the seating. I do not wish to boast, but I have heard it said that men still talk in Oxford about the verve and authority I brought to the hiring of chairs and van alike.

I retired from the theatre soon after that. I used to go to see Oxford productions quite often, though. Even now, almost twenty years on, I am unable to watch Gordon Honeycombe read the *News At Ten* without recalling the magic experience of his Othello. As the trade figures spill impeccably from his lips, I cannot forbear from expecting him, any second now, to break into 'Sonny Boy'.

It was by now the summer of 1958, and in the various water-

ways around Oxford the punts coagulated sluggishly into log-
jams as their polers hove to in order to read aloud to one
another.

Through the mists of spiralling gnat, snatches of Salinger
and Scott Fitzgerald filtered from boat to boat: the fashions
that summer were *The Catcher In The Rye*, *The Great Gatsby*
(resurrected by some nostalgic spirit at the Bodley Head),
Lord Of The Flies, *The Alexandria Quartet* (or, rather, trilogy;
Clea still writhed in Durrell s churning head, accreting met-
aphor) and *Our Man In Havana*. These were the mass-consump-
tion biggies, though a few rarer souls had forked out their
fifteen-bobs on Iris Murdoch's *The Bell* and Angus Wilson's
The Middle Age of Mrs Eliot. Almost everyone had bought
Doctor Zhivago, though it would have been possible to put all
those who had actually finished it into one punt with no
threat whatever to buoyancy.

It was primarily in consequence of Salinger's brush-fire
success that some ninety-five per cent of the people one met
that summer were writing novels. Why it had taken five years
for the book to catch on I have no idea; all I do know is that
in Wadham it was impossible to sleep at night for the clatter
of Olivettis reverberating around the Old Quad, scattering
Jacobean shards onto the unconscious drunks beneath, and I
have no reason to believe other colleges were any quieter. All
the novels got as far as page forty-one and contained much
iridescent description of blackhead and bra-strap; it was as if
Salinger were some kind of Pied Piper whose fanatical followers
disappeared into the rock at page forty-one.

Wadham contained two energetic typists who actually
managed to complete whole novels, and, what is more, get
them published: David Caute and Julian Mitchell released
their *oeuvres* to a slavering world, and the London agent
became overnight a permanent ornament to the Oxford scene.
In the embering 'fifties, it was impossible to go to a literary
party without finding a pin-striped man from A. D. Peters or
Curtis Brown leaning on the mantelpiece with the easy non-

chalance that betokens the small fish in an even smaller pool and eyeing the bustier nurses while passionate literati informed him that they were currently engaged upon a revolutionary prose project that would make Henry James stand on his ear.

And then there was poetry, or Dom Moraes, as it came to be called. Dom's success having carried beyond the city limits, he was the focus of much ambivalent admiration: I recall in particular one occasion upon which he rushed in to inform the aforementioned J. Mitchell, who also assumed he wrote poetry, that a London actress—having found herself in the Moraes chambers with their tenant unaccountably absent and possibly escorting some other lady—had torn up all his manuscripts. There came into Mitchell's kindly eyes an odd light that, had it been spotted by le Duc de la Rochefoucauld might well have sent the old aristo scurrying off to write 'Dans l'adversité de nos meilleurs amis, nous trouvons quelque chose qui ne nous déplaît pas.' But, then, he was not there, so the moment will have to be allowed to pass into literary history without benefit of speculation.

It was soon after this that Julian and I went into the movie business together. Seeing himself, I believe, as some kind of Wykehamist Sacha Guitry, Julian temporarily laid aside his various careers as scholar, poet, novelist, journalist and wit in favour of searching for fresh fields to be conquered on. He bought an old 16mm Bolex and several miles of black-and-white stock, and invited me to be the cameraman to the *nouvelle vague* with which he intended to engulf Oxford, and, indeed, the world.

Film had become very big with the intelligentsia by then. It was always referred to unarticled, as in 'That is what film is all about', 'Antonioni has, how shall I put it, a *sense* of film,' and so on, and at the Scala Cinema in Walton Street, anyone who cared anything about film would flock to the latest epic examination of trauma on the Scandinavian foreshore. Directors became currency, as once stars had been; subjects were irrelevant: 'I thought we might see a Bergman and have a curry afterwards' was, by 1959, the most familiar phrase in the English language.

Now, had the good Ingmar never existed, nor Fellini and Buñuel, there is every chance that Mitchell and I might have made quite a decent little documentary about that area of working-class Oxford called Jericho. Indeed, I thought that's what we *were* making: we would potter the streets in Julian's old Morris Minor, whacking away at characterful faces, broken windows, derelict churches, all that fraught stuff, and by the end of the month, I personally reckoned we had enough poignant footage to persuade Cartier Bresson to chuck in the towel and open a tobacconist's.

But when we came to cut the thing and edit it (at a charming Cheyne Walk house gutted to make a film factory by its owner, the excitable Jeremy Sandford), it became clear to me that what Julian had believed we were making was an agglomeration of *Citizen Kane*, *Le Chien Andalou* and *Alexander Nevski*.

With every pretension complete, it was sent to the Edinburgh Festival, where, according to Julian (I had by this time walked away from the carnage), it was Mentioned. In what terms it was Mentioned I dare not begin to guess, though references to Old Bolex were doubtless rife, if I'm any judge of the low level of cinematic wit.

'Of course, there's always journalism' was a phrase that rang round the neighbourhood, I recall. Its first peal tended to echo the clack as the Olivetti typed 42 at the top of a virgin sheet, announcing that the novel had come to its premature (yet inevitable) end, and its author hurled the machine aside the better to assume the pose of poor Chatterton conked out on his ottoman. Literary snobbery being what it was, is, and doubtless always will be, failed novelists invariably expect that when their Muse gathers her soft skirts and runs, the Fleet

Street whore will slide from her doorway and grab them to her withered dugs with the hungry gratitude of all unloved things.

That this never happens demonstrates only that most aspirant novelists know as little about life as they do about writing. But, in Oxford, at least, their arrogance had a certain naive charm.

'I suppose I could always do the Ken Tynan/Bernard Levin/ Nick Tomalin stuff', the lovely lads would sigh irritably; and would then hightail it into Oxford journalism where they immediately gave evidence that if any subsequent newspaper let them nearer anything more challenging than the local flower show, it could mean only that their father had been at school with the paper's proprietor.

Basically, there were, in those days, three sorts of under-graduate journal: there was *Cherwell*, a news-sheet which misspelt the wrong information and then illustrated it with a photograph of something else printed upside down; there was *Isis*, a literary magazine packed with verse so free you couldn't even give it away and short stories about people staring at cracks in the ceiling while they waited for the abortionist to ring; and there were Little Magazines, called *Boil* and *Fart* and so on, most of which owed so much to Allen Ginsberg that if they ever paid the old fraud back he'd have enough oaths to keep a town the size of Cleveland swearing until well into the next century.

I myself had some considerable success with *Isis* during 1959, mainly on the strength of a donkey jacket I had purchased second-hand in a Folly Bridge pawnshop, an accent that went with it, and a habit I cultivated of cracking my knuckles, narrowing my eyes to slits, and spitting tobacco pips out with no concern for targets. Thus it was that I became an authentic working-class voice, and sold many stories to a succession of gentlemanly editors each of whom was allowed to believe he had discovered Frank Norman alive and well and living in the Thames Valley. That I secretly committed *Brideshead Revisited* to memory while listening to Albinoni in a mustard

quilted housecoat was, of course, information that never went
beyond the joss-choked dig in which it happened.

There was also at that time a curious journalistic operation
in progress, cobbled together by a small group of prep-school
japesmiths who had latched on to the immortal truth that if
they said 'bum' or 'nigger' often enough, they could make one
another fall down and roll helpless on the Axminster. In order
to bring this illimitable delight to a wider world, they founded
a magazine called *Parson's Pleasure*. It subsequently became
Private Eye, where it has gone from weakness to weakness.

I seem, here and there in this chronicle of gelded youth, to
have hinted that class still ran its fading blue thread through
the social woof of Oxford.

And so it did, albeit oddly.

For in these, the immediate post-Angry years, new heroes and
new hierarchies had burgeoned, overgrowing the old. New
prides were everywhere, which in turn meant new arrogances
and vanities, which in their turn meant new pretensions and
deceptions. One was constantly bumping into people who
referred to themselves as one, blushed, and corrected the
offending emblem to *you*. Tall willowy lads with inbred conks
and hyphens might be found, in the dead of any night, burning
their cavalry twills and chukka boots in lay-bys along the A40,
thereafter changing into blue jeans and Marks woollies. They
stood before mirrors, abbreviating their drawls and lopping
their aitches; they defended, with a heartbreaking desperation,
their entitlement to membership of the new order.

Thus:

'Yes, well, I mean werl, my father, that is to say me dad,
did send me to Stowe, but that doesn't, don't, mean I'm one of
your mindless bleeding plutocracy'.

Or:

'I'm not saying the family aren't merchant bankers *now*, I'm
only trying to point out that in the early fourteenth century

they were all solidly behind Wat Tyler. I mean, bugger me, squire, there's nowt tha can teach me about t'working-class struggle, tha knows!'

And:

'Oh God, roll on my twenty-first, I'll be able to renounce my title and just be plain Auberon Fitzwilliam de Brissac Giles Corkseeping-ffearfful!'

But there were still, you may be amazed to hear, a few glaring class indicants; and the most interesting of these, or certainly the one most fraught with ramification, was sexual. It was a general principle among privately educated male undergraduates that one walked about holding hands with well-born gels whom one planned eventually to marry, but screwed nurses; whereas the rest of us walked about holding hands with nurses whom we planned eventually to marry, and screwed well-born gels. Oxford could be said to divide along a Lord Chatterley/Oliver Mellors line; and it really was the most super fun, as we used to say to the supine ruins as we reached for our shoes and detached the bicycle clips from our fallen underwear. It was like being a member of some sexual fifth column, dare I say crack division, dropped into alien territory to infiltrate and sabotage.

I myself was less conscious than many of the lads of the political implications of pleasure. I have heard that there *were* blokes who, at fever pitch in the cloistered confines of some curtained St Anne's eyrie, shouted to their panting ex-Roedean victim: 'And this one's for Jarrow!', though I cannot swear to the accuracy of the report.

What was certain was that these were interesting sexual times. It was the period of, if you like, the phoney permissive war, a time of promiscuous false alarms, and daring border raids, and wild rumour, and occasional staggering achievements by bold pioneers. Undergraduates could, for example, still be sent down for being caught *in flagrante delicto*, but this did not stop some of them from pulling coups which, had they known about them, would have sent college authorities scurrying to the statute books to seek among the footnotes a precedent for garrotting. I recall one particular occasion on which a Wadham friend, a studious introverted lad with a passion only for (or so we imagined) chess, took two foreign girls from the St Giles School of English to his room in the Wren Building and kept them there for five days. We learned of this ongoing tryst only on the fourth day, when, unable any longer to contain our speculation, we stopped him on what had become one of his regular journeys between the JCR bar and his quarters with teetering platefuls of tomato sandwiches, to enquire the reason for this sudden Vitamin C craving.

He revealed to us that one of the girls was Portuguese, the other Norwegian, and that both of them had enrolled only the week before. None of the three spoke the language of any of the others. I never learned what subsequently became of the girls (the hero returned to his chess and introspection on the sixth day), but I still, even today, occasionally divert myself with thoughts of what they must have made of this induction into English mores.

Do they still tell their goggle-eyed co-nationals of that strange race of pasty troilists beyond the foam who subsist entirely on tomatoes and are content to communicate only from loin to loin?

I do not propose to dwell upon the many deep and meaningful and very, very wonderful relationships I shared, and where I could not share enjoyed, in those distant days. All the girls were, Oxford being the lusty pastoral idyll it was, extra-ordinarily beautiful, brilliantly witty, by turns tender and inventive, passionate and sophisticated: in short, successive amalgams of Zuleika Dobson, Zelda Fitzgerald, Princess Casamassima and Catherine the Great, particularly a wonderfully vital young seat-trimmer from Morris Motors who was Beatrice to my Dante for nearly a week in early 1960, who had a bust you could stand carriage-clocks on, and who is selected to represent her fortunate sorority in this narrative only because of the interesting sidelight she helps throw upon the shifting moral shadows of the time.

I was living in digs on the Iffley Road that spring, with a Mr and Mrs Fairless, a kind hardworking couple in their late thirties, who had four children and a budgerigar that was encouraged to fly round the breakfast room, walk through one's cornflakes, and enquire at repetitive length what one thought of his prettiness.

The Fairlesses were in the habit of retiring at around 10 pm, enabling anyone with a lissom seat-trimmer on his hands to introduce her to more comfortable premises before the sword outwore the sheath; and for several nights, much that life has to offer had its options taken up in that quiet Victorian semi, the seat-trimmer departing with the dawn.

Except, that is, for the night on which she overslept and, tripping down the hall, fetched up against assorted Fairlesses homing in on bacon. I lay listening to the formal exchanges and the slam of the front-door; no plausible excuses sprang into the mind, so I prepared myself to brazen out whatever lay ahead, washed, shaved, and went in to breakfast.

The meal passed reasonably enough, any stases in the conversation being ably taken care of by child and bird, and it was not until their mother took the children out to hose them down for school that I found myself alone with the landlord. As in some bizarre parody of Victorian melodrama, he paced the linoleum awhile before turning. At last:

'Look here,' he said, 'I think I ought to make it clear that—'

It was at this point that the budgie landed on my head.

'Go away, Charlie,' said the landlord.

'I'm so nice,' said Charlie. 'I'm so nice.'

'Here's a fine do,' said the landlord.

'Go away, Charlie,' I said.

This pre-emptive strike having been taken by the bird, the landlord's iron jut went limp.

'About this young lady,' he said.

'Yes?' I said.

'I hope you're going steady,' he said.

I realize I have said very little about work.

This is primarily because in the matters of study and intent, I doubt that my generation was very different from any other Oxford generation, the undergraduate corps being split into those who looked upon the university as an opportunity for general enlightenment, unshackled to the mundane pursuit of mere honours and qualifications, i.e. those who got drunk a lot and fell off walls after midnight; and those who looked upon it as the finest centre for formal education in all the world where, in the lush environment of scholarship and mature enthusiasms for eliciting one's fullest potential, the brilliant student would become tomorrow's titan, i.e. those who had four ball-point pens of different colours in their white lab-coats and subsequently vanished into ICI.

As a cross-cultural utilitarian bohemian who dreamt of carrying off the Nobel Prize for Literature while at the same time holding down a steady pensionable position with luncheon vouchers, I tended to straddle these schemata, at considerable perineal risk. Fortunately for me, I was reading English, a discipline hardly worthy the title, involving as it did nothing more arduous than sitting under a tree and reading books that one would otherwise have read for pleasure, and, at the end of three years, showing off about them to grown-ups.

There was, of course, Anglo-Saxon, which formed a mandatory part of English Schools just in order to endow the course with a spurious scholasticism; but where others carped constantly at having to wrestle with yog and thorn, I really rather enjoyed *learning* something at Oxford. Especially something with no use, purpose, or practical application whatever. My only sadness in the Old English course came with the discovery that *The Battle of Maldon* was but a fragment: hardly has Aelfwine, son of Aelfric, mounted his counter-attack than the manuscript comes to its mouse-chewed end. What the final score-line was, we shall never know.

In short, then, what Oxford did was train me to understand that true happiness in life attended that man who could persuade someone to pay him to work at something which he would otherwise do from love, anyway. And that, therefore, is the course to which I have cleaved for the past sixteen years, with much joy.

Martin Amis

Martin Amis was born in 1949, a son of Kingsley Amis. He was educated in Britain, Spain and the United States, attending over thirteen schools and then a series of crammers in London and Brighton. He gained a formal first in English at Exeter College. After leaving Oxford, he worked for three years as an editorial assistant on The Times Literary Supplement, and is now assistant literary editor of the New Statesman. He has published two novels, The Rachel Papers (1973) and Dead Babies (1975), and a number of short stories.

My Oxford is likely to seem rather shapeless—even rather jangling and unassimilated—compared to reports of it by my predecessors there. This is because my Oxford, the Oxford of 1968–71 (and presumably everyone else's Oxfords thereafter), did not feel like an experience which had shape, point, a clear structural place in one's life. I'd better add quickly that it was, for me, often a terrifying, hilarious and emotionally eventful three years, but I suspect that, for me, those years would have been terrifying, hilarious and emotionally eventful anyway.

Oxford is no longer somewhere with a special focus and a special identity: it is just somewhere that gets passed through by individuals. There will, for example, be no more Oxford 'generations'; eminent contemporaries may emerge, they may even happen to have known each other, but all sense of cultural community is gone, for better or for worse. Socially—in the sense of trying to make friends and trying to fall in love with certain people—it is as easy or as difficult as your social life ever is: with more varied opportunities, but no easier. And intellectually, too, it is for the most part a collection of people sitting alone in rooms, one of whom turns out to be you.

When I went up to Oxford I was anticipating just this— anticipating just everything, really: far and away the most flamboyant and original things about my Oxford were my presuppositions about the place. What the hell would I do? I knew, for a start, that only two types of people ever went to Oxford, and I knew, for a fact, that I belonged to neither. I was not (i) a craven swot from somewhere called Heaptown, so I wouldn't be picking my nails with a compass and drinking quarts of instant coffee in my room all day, joining the Young Trade Unionists, going to Venezuelan films at the cinema clubs, talking about politics, engineering and jobs, and (if I was lucky) getting my terrified girl-friend down from home every other weekend. Equally, I was not (ii) a haughty cretin from one of our public schools, so I wouldn't be motoring my 1898 MG into the country for strawberry picnics, joining the Young Reactionaries, debagging new boys and roasting town yobs, beating the daylights out of the Junior Common Rooms after Cuppers Suppers, putting chamber pots and cars on chapel spires, and falling for the fresher on the next staircase.

No, I was a Londoner, thanks, far too flash and worldly to countenance the pompous hicks and dumb Henries I expected to find in boring old Oxford. For instance, I could account constructively for only *five days* of the traditional mind-expanding nine months between school and university, in which I had worked in my step-uncle's record shop in Rickmansworth —whereas, I imagined, the hicks had all gained key positions in blacking factories and the Henries had all walked from Oslo to Peking and back. Oxford would just be where I went to work, for the almost derisory eight-week terms. I wouldn't need to know anyone; I did not want to act, edit, debate, row or run; I would be a loner, a poet, a dreamer. London would always be there, waiting to be rediscovered by me—and I had even decided coolly to return to it for the first weekend of term.

Underwriting these excitable notions, of course, was an element of candid terror. Originally a child of the lower middle classes, I feared what I so lazily disdained, and in the same over-heated terms. Again, I could see it all. Three years of unsuccessfully dodging streetfights, waking up on the quad lawn in my underpants, getting my velvet suit slashed and my tiny hi-fi stomped in, hiding under my sofa as, outside, loutish Yahooism raged along the staircases. Or alternatively, three years of waking up every morning dangling naked from the chapel rafters, my head shaved, my balls blackened with shoe polish, and a sign reading 'Yaroo—College Squit!' suspended from my neck. And—anyway—would I be *clever* enough . . . all those wizened ghouls on *University Challenge*—they may have looked like Bamber Gascoigne's uncles, but boy did they know their shit. I'd obviously have to work like an idiot to avoid instant disgrace and expulsion, never mind girls, friends, London, meals, sleep, anything. I imagined myself studying away in dour and dusty solitude, while the rest of the world clamoured gaily somewhere out of doors, coming to my ears like the sound of street footfalls to children sent to bed early in summer.

As if in deft reply to these academico-social misgivings, I checked in on the Saturday before term started at Exeter College, Oxford—to find that I was sharing rooms with an Old Harrovian who said 'Pardon?' when he meant 'What?'! Everything about this arrangement mortified me: the matching desks symmetrically flanking the bar heater in our large and uncompanionable sitting-room (no truly humane scholarship, surely, could ever be done there); the matching, cream-walled bed-cubicles leading off it (no Oxford girl, surely, could ever be successfully entertained there); and the goofy horror of my 'room-mate' (as disgusted by my presence, surely, as I was by his). If I was going to suffer, I thought to myself, I wanted to suffer on my own, not with a fellow-dud lurching and fumbling alongside me. Anyhow, three weeks later, having completed a gauntlet of routine grotesqueries—eighty-four hours with Roget on my lap writing my first essay, lone sconce-dreading dinners in hall (i.e. college), a begowned sampling of lectures and libraries, tentative, don't-mind-me sorties into the town—I got a credulous Classicist to swap his room for my half of mine. Then I started to look round about me.

Although more fragmented and less corny than I had expected, there *were* types of people at Oxford, and like all types they elected to stick together. In some senses, also, my slanderous fancies about them had not been altogether without foundation. Galumphing Henries with diagonal pock-marked faces (people who would starve to death if locked in a fully-equipped kitchen) were well enough represented; my Harrovian room-mate said that, on his visits to Oriel, he felt as though he had wandered back to Harrow, such was the incidence of closed-scholarship dunces who groped and blinked through its quads. And the out-of-towner owls were very much about the place too: at the end of a gluttonous college breakfast (one of the real joys of Oxford life), during which I had talked Talleyrand with an unsmiling rustic, I asked him why he was filling his pockets with marmalade rolls. 'For the girlfriend,' he said, gesturing with his head to indicate the hungry room where she damply cowered.

But there were more types than I had thought there would be, and they weren't, in my view, sufficiently well-defined or demarcated types, and I wasn't quite clear which type *I* was or how I could change types and become one of their types even supposing I wanted to. Which type, anyway?

There were political people (you seemed to need a ginger beard to be one of them); they came to your room for talks or tried to sell you scabrous hate-sheets in the quad; they fought for valorous reforms like having breakfast served fifteen minutes later, and they picketed the innocuous Matriculation ceremony (one cleverly ironic graffito at the time was MATRICULATION MAKES YOU BLIND); they also staged an angry meeting about the invasion of Czechoslovakia in my first term, which I angrily attended. There were a few God people left—another dying breed; they came to your room, too, but with such queasy diffidence that you could quite often just tell them to go away. There were sport people, who seemed to keep themselves agreeably to themselves, apart from self-destructive rampages after some important date in their calendar.

There was a great deal of what were called 'gnome' people;
almost brazenly repulsive in dress, demeanour and visage,
these humble clerks of the new literacy stuck in groups of four
and five, attended lectures during the morning and libraries
in the afternoon, invariably enjoyed dinner in college (legend
told of a gnome who never once signed out for dinner in his
entire four-year course), and, still in a clump, quaffed Bournvita
well into the large hours. And then there were the 'cool'
people (a fairly recent type, I should think), the aloof, slightly
moneyed, London-based, car-driving, party-throwing, even
vaguely intellectual butterfly elite; I say with confidence that
they had among their number all the cockiest and best-
looking youths in Oxford; they drank alcohol and took drugs,
and they were as promiscuous as anyone well could be there;
in many ways they seemed to be having the best time.

Oddly, incongruously (and probably not at all, really), I
seemed to straddle these last two types. I had no friends, no
friends whatever; a potent qualification for gnome membership.
I did indeed drink a lot of instant coffee, spending in aggregate
(I would guess) the equivalent of a term crouched over my
electric kettle. I always ate in hall and always tried to stay
close to my old room-mate and his new one, a delightful pair.
I, of course, had no girlfriend. All I had was a room. In fact,
even during my relatively in-demand periods at Oxford, most
of my life there was to consist of me alone in a study, reading
books pressed calmly out on the blotting-paper, or writing
malarial, pageant-like, all-night essays, or listening to records,
or playing moronically simple forms of patience, or having
soul-sessions, or having crying-jags. And, however self-pitying
I was about it at the time, this segment of my life I regret not
at all: a relative late-comer to literature, I was a contrite
pilgrim on the path towards its discovery. Many poignant and
humbling moments were passed with assorted masterpieces
staked out on my lap; over those three years 'the friction, the
sense of pregnant arrest' which accompanies fresh intimacy
with an *oeuvre* (the glamorous phrase is F. R. Leavis's) was a

regular guest at Tower 1, my romantic room facing the stained glass of the chapel windows ten yards opposite, which were warmly illuminated from within at dusk.

And yet—come, come—I wanted a good time too: and there I was, in my black velvet suit, my snakeskin boots and eagerly patterned shirt, a relative tike by Oxford standards, with quite a few metropolitan girlfriends and one metropolitan love-affair under my belt, a famous Oxonian father, hardly a perfect stranger to human contact, not unpleasing (though small) to look at, a £9-a-week allowance—and nothing to do. I wanted friends, and I wanted to be loved, same as any other undergraduate. I wanted friends because I wanted a girlfriend. But I couldn't have a girlfriend because I didn't have any friends.

So most of my leisure during the first term was single-mindedly devoted to one activity: not getting a girlfriend. I spent several hours every day of the week all over Oxford not getting a girlfriend. In the bookshops I would not get a girl-friend by wandering along the shelves, standing as near as I dared to them and not engaging them in conversation. In the streets I did not get them by walking silently past them. In the libraries, not getting a girlfriend took the form of sitting opposite them and not sending them notes. I joined the Poetry Society (thinking, for some reason or other, that Poetry Society girls would be, by definition, both beautiful and sexually un-discriminating) and did not get a girlfriend at the few meetings I attended, during which plain persons of both sexes un-blushingly read out their own verse, or unblushingly sat about while others read out theirs. (In addition, and equipped with similar motives, I joined the Humanist Society, which was also very horrible, and particularly good for not getting girl-friends at.) Least taxing of all, perhaps, was not getting a girlfriend in the lecture hall; one just stared across it at them.

Two things about Oxford girls seemed immediately clear: first, that you could never be happy there without one, and, second, that there was no means of ever getting to know one.

And by 'Oxford girls' I mean all the girls in Oxford, not just those clever, serious, independent students, the ones with more O-levels than freckles on their faces, who looked as if they had just cycled 'up' from Cheltenham or Tunbridge Wells, and who (one imagined) would not take to being stuttered at in the streets. As I staggered through the town on those hollow autumn afternoons, directing my gaze impartially at town and gown alike, it was not for a Zuleika Dobson, nor even for a Jill, that I craved: what I craved for was a girl—or someone who knew one, or someone who knew someone who knew one.

Which posed problems for Oxford's reply to Albert Camus, the Kafka of Carfax, who had serenely redirected the few offers of companionship he had received. After half a term at Oxford I think I am right in saying that, throughout the entire borough, I knew one human being—not counting my ex-room-mate (by now I had abandoned my former haughtiness and perpetually ached to be by his side), my 'scout' (or cleaning-man—a menacing and thyroid-eyed Welshman), and my tutor (urbane, pooh-poohing Jonathan Wordsworth, the distinguished nepotic scholar). This other human being I knew was shy, at Balliol, and, incidentally, was the son of the then Minister of Defence, now custodian of our economy. *He* already had a girlfriend, a metropolitan one whom I vaguely knew, who in turn knew another female human being, an Oxford-based one, whom I sometimes came across when I saw them together. With this young lady giving me nothing whatever in the way of encouragement—save that she showed no sign of unrealistically abrupt dislike—my prolix and gawky approach-work began.

My introductory period at Oxford, then, was given over (a) to work for preliminary exams, and (b) to not getting this particular girl. The first was solitary, satisfying, sane; the second expensive, nerve-racking, and wealthy in embarrassment.

We saw films two or three nights a week and—to my secret boredom—attended the odd meeting or discussion or talk (a nomadic sampler of secretarial courses at the time, she later went on to read Philosophy at London). I held her hand now and then. We ate in College whenever possible, because it was free, or we ate in a friendly Wimpy Bar opposite St John's, because it was cheap. On a few occasions she suffered me to kiss her goodnight at the bus stop. Things continued not to improve. One night in her flat she went through the pockets of my jacket (under my supervision) in search of some matches. I died a little as she accidentally produced a wallet of contraceptives instead. 'Well, you never know your luck,' I said.

And I certainly never knew mine, throughout that Michaelmas term—though I remained deeply convinced that this was all somehow better than nothing. I called at the lady's London home once or twice during the Christmas vacation—which I divided between hard work, light revelry, and sitting about waiting for her passionate, Lawrentian, slightly pornographic (and actually non-existent) letters. In London I assume I cut a rather more attractive figure, what with my stepmother's smart yellow car and my own relative aplomb in the metropolis. But Oxford, the true locus of both our lives then, was the place in which the battle would be lost or won, and I was impatient to return there, after the yawning six-week recess, in the new year. (I later learned, interestingly, that my non-girlfriend had beguiled the vac by having an affair with someone else— and someone who everybody agreed was much nastier, thicker and uglier than me.)

Early on in my second term the election for the Oxford Professorship of Poetry was held. My father, as an M.A. (and an implacable foe of Yevgeny Yevtushenko), had come up to vote for Roy Fuller, whose son John threw a party. I was asked along—and I sexily invited my non-girlfriend along too. She embraced this opportunity to make her indifference known, and I returned to my room *à un*, realizing that after half a year in this life-enhancing, character-building, horizon-expanding place, I now had no one, nothing. The famous skylines I could see from my window, the stained-glass hagiographies of the

chapel opposite, the Songs and Sonnets of John Donne laid out
tenderly on my desk—suddenly all this was second-hand, mere
leftovers, junk. I sat there for several hours, and when I
couldn't bear sitting down I stood up, and when I couldn't
bear standing up I sat down. About 9 o'clock there was a tap
on the door. It was she, bearing apologies and a persuasively-
worded invitation to return with her to her flat. Intimacy (with
the author in rather less than colossal form) took place, and a
happy few months began.

As against this—and hardly less rollickingly—I was working
with paranoid verve for Prelims, unpleasant and meaningless
exams which befall the student at the end of his or her second
term. The five papers include one on Old English grammar, all
indecipherable inflection changes and vile vowel movements,
and a Latin paper, requiring from the candidate two translations from Books IV and VI of the *Aeneid*. (Both these papers
have been superseded; mine was the last year to sit them, for
which many thanks.) In my Oxford entrance papers, my
attempt at the Latin unseen had consisted of a single word, mis-
translated: I had rendered *igitur* as 'the general', whereas I
gather it in fact means 'therefore'. Well, *igitur* I now took the
precaution of memorizing literal translations of these two books
in their entirety. (This would raise only two dangers: not
recognizing the passages, and not knowing, as it were, when to
stop translating them.) Towards the end I worked practically
round the clock. I used to leave notes by my alarm—often set
for 4 or 5 am—saying things like *Oh Really Get Up* and BLOODY
GET UP! in case I merely slapped the button and returned
groaning to my cot. I worked far, far too hard, and passed
with jittery ease. When the exams ended so, for some logical-
seeming reason, did my interest in the girl whom I had courted
and squired for nearly a year.

And that's how it went on, I'm afraid. I was lucky enough
to get another girlfriend, a connection which bestrode the
(traditionally quite idle) second year and flourished well into
the third. Under this girlfriend's auspices—she was a History

freshwoman whom I had known a bit before she came up—my social needle's-eye expanded somewhat, and I tasted some of the conventional sweets of Oxonian life. Punting drunkenly up the Isis to a hostelry at evening, being tweely offered a choice of Malvern Water and tonic at a 'drinks' party on the beautiful lake-side lawn at Worcester College, walking round the place with my father (all husky with nostalgia—but then he had a Generation to talk to when he was there) on his infrequent visits, stealing the odd drug from the trusting, ponderous pushers at Hertford, rather shining in classes with my derivative and journalistic essays, going to many films many times, smuggling the St Hilda's scholar past the scout on my staircase, feeling superior to new boys, getting a bigger room, having more interesting periods to study . . . till Finals loomed.

Nobody can be forced to work at Oxford, but things are made easy, pleasant and stimulating for those who want to work. And just as there is the time for pleasure, there is the time for boredom and neurosis, which only work can fill. At the beginning of my third year, owing to an impetuous scheme to share a house in the country with unstable and profligate friends, work was fatally eased out by pleasure, most of it pleasureless, and for my last two terms I radically readjusted— i.e., over-readjusted, as usual.

In short, I re-embraced the life of a gnome. Leaving the house and the girlfriend in equally disgraceful circumstances, I moved into the Annexe of my college, a grim bastion of gnomery on the unattractive Iffley Road. It was a large flat house that smelled of locker rooms and lavatory spray, a suspended, echoic warren of shuffling caretakers, winded cats and dozens of progeriac postgraduates, who resembled very old ladies and who made fantastically elaborate meals for themselves three times a day, and sat about all the time discussing those meals, either anticipatorily, or with the evaluating calm of hindsight. It suited me perfectly.

Here I went again: I rose at 6 am, drank a great deal of

coffee ('real' coffee by now), worked until 8, went into college
for breakfast, took my seat in the college library by 8.45,
worked until 1, had lunch in college, took my seat in the
college library by 1.45, worked until 7, returned to the Iffley
Road, worked until 9, prepared for myself a Vesta Beef Curry
or a Vesta Chicken Supreme or—best—a Vesta Paella (not
a single item of genuine nutriment, I can safely boast, passed
down my throat at Exeter House), returned to my desk and
worked until 1 am. I rose at 6 am . . . At this rate, I was going
to look a bit of a bloody fool if I didn't do very well indeed.
The nine three-hour papers came in a heroic blur. I got a
formal First, coming third in that year.

The unique freedom of Oxford—now more than ever,
probably—is that you don't have to account for more than,
say, ninety minutes a week for eighteen weeks a year. That's
about three days out of three years of your life. Conventional
ways of filling that time are gone; it is all yours now. It doesn't
happen to you before and it never happens to you again.
Perhaps once is enough—but not more than enough.

A. J. SHERMAN